The Unstoppable Christian Business

THE UNSTOPPABLE CHRISTIAN BUSINESS

7 STEPS TO YOUR 7 FIGURE BUSINESS WITH PURPOSE, PASSION, AND PROFIT

DR. RON ECCLES
"THE SUCCESS DOCTOR"

NEW YORK

LONDON • NASHVILLE • MELBOURNE • VANCOUVER

The Unstoppable Christian Business

7 Steps to Your 7 Figure Business with Purpose, Passion, and Profit

Published in New York, New York, by Morgan James Publishing. Morgan James is a trademark of Morgan James, LLC. www.MorganJamesPublishing.com

Proudly distributed by Ingram Publisher Services.

Please visit www.DrRonEccles.com for more information on my coaching programs and speaking opportunities. Email me at DrRon@DrRonEccles.com.

A **FREE** ebook edition is available for you or a friend with the purchase of this print book.

CLEARLY SIGN YOUR NAME ABOVE

Instructions to claim your free ebook edition:
1. Visit MorganJamesBOGO.com
2. Sign your name CLEARLY in the space above
3. Complete the form and submit a photo of this entire page
4. You or your friend can download the ebook to your preferred device

ISBN 9781631957635 paperback
ISBN 9781631957642 ebook
Library of Congress Control Number: 2021946408

Cover and Interior Design by:
Chris Treccani
www.3dogcreative.net

Morgan James is a proud partner of Habitat for Humanity Peninsula and Greater Williamsburg. Partners in building since 2006.

Get involved today! Visit MorganJamesPublishing.com/giving-back

To My Lord and Savior Jesus Christ,
there are no words to express my love and
gratitude for the grace and mercy you poured
out for me on the Cross.

To my Dad and Mom (Ronald and Marie) for
always loving and believing in me.

To my wife, Johanna, you are the wind in my
sails, my lover, my heart, and my best friend.

To my children, Luke, Carissa, Angelena,
Patrick, and Jade, I am proud to be your Dad.

To my G-Children, Mateo and Valentina, your
smile fills me with joy unimaginable.

To my sisters, Anne, Marylou, and Debbie, I am
grateful for you in my life.

To my family and friends, you have impacted
my life in great ways.

The primary purpose of business is to make disciples.

The second is to make massive profit.

TABLE OF CONTENTS

NOTE TO THE READER

WHAT YOU WILL BENEFIT FROM READING THIS BOOK

NOTHING! That's correct. I said it.

My friend James Malinchak is the best teacher/trainer I know on how to build a great business as a professional speaker (*www.BigMoneySpeaker. com*). James is also a highly sought-after speaker because of his high-energy, entertaining style and rock-solid content. He is famous for always teaching that knowledge is only *potential* power for transformational growth. Real growth through transformation happens when you take knowledge and PUT IT INTO *ACTION*!

I'll make you this promise: When you read the lessons contained in this book and you commit to taking daily action through *implementation*, you will set yourself up for growth in your personal and business life. A growth that is *Kingdom-purpose driven.*

The ultimate goal of this book is to transform you and your business. My plan is to help you leverage the platform God has given you for the primary purpose of making disciples, and secondarily, making maximum profit. And all for His Glory.

HOW TO READ THIS BOOK

This book contains three sections that all work together to help you build a solid foundation for scalable growth with fewer headaches. The goal is to master the principles laid out in order to achieve the outcomes you desire.

I suggest reading this book several times and consider joining one of my coaching programs if you want faster growth.

WHY YOU SHOULD READ AND APPLY THE PRINCIPLES DESCRIBED IN THIS BOOK

Imagine you're traveling on a road and you come across a large field you need to cross. Written on a large sign is "CAUTION—LAND MINES." You're unsure of what to do; you want to get to the other side, but you don't want to get blown up!

Suddenly, on the other side of the field you see a person. They shout across the field to you asking if you want to cross. You say yes.

They respond that they can help you to get to your destination safely since they have crossed this field many times before and know where all the land mines are buried; however, there will be a cost involved.

You're faced with three choices:

- One, stay where you're at.

- Two, attempt to cross on your own and chance getting wounded or killed.

- Three, pay the fee and safely and *successfully* make it to the other side.

THE CHOICE IS YOURS!

PREFACE

I wrote this book so that business owners would have the necessary understanding of "What to Do" in order to wisely build a massively profitable business that is driven by *PURPOSE*.

Since 1983, I have owned and operated multiple six- and seven-figure businesses. My professional career started as a Doctor of Chiropractic with advanced degrees in orthopedics, neurology, and sports injury.

Over the past three-plus decades, I have taught postgraduate courses for several chiropractic universities, owned and operated multiple restaurants, and developed expertise investing in real estate.

It was around 2009 that I started my current passion as a professional speaker and working with business owners as a consultant, mentor, and coach.

Every part of my journey in the past 37 years prepared me for my calling today: to help equip business owners to quickly build extremely profitable businesses with purpose.

My wife, Johanna, and I launched Unstoppable Christian (*www.facebook.com/UnstoppableChristianWorldwide/*) in 2017 to encourage believers throughout the world, and ROAR (*www.theROARevent.com*), in 2018, to help Christian Business Owners maximize their business and personal lives with Kingdom purpose.

I enjoyed great successes and made many mistakes along the way; some had a higher cost than others.

My greatest mistake was the posture on my heart.

For decades, I was building my financial empire and sometimes giving God His 10 percent (Tithe). I emphasize the words *I* and *me* because it identifies the root issue.

It took me close to 30 years to finally come to grips that NONE of my success was of my doing.

Every breath, every heartbeat, every gift, all my drive and passion was GOD GIVEN. It was all His, and I was the servant assigned as the steward of it.

Once I understood this, my heart and focus changed. My job was to faithfully seek the will of the Father, through the direction of the Holy Spirit, each day for "Kingdom Purposes."

For every Christian that has a business, our first focus (or purpose) is to make disciples.

I now spend my energies on inspiring, empowering, and coaching men and women like you to reach your full God-given potential in life and business.

The following story was inspired by a 1988 song by Ray Boltz, "Thank You for Giving to The Lord." It's a reminder for us to keep our focus on the most important things on this side of heaven.

THE THREE PEOPLE I MET IN HEAVEN

One night, I had a dream that filled me with unimaginable joy.

I dreamed I was escorted to the Gates of Heaven by an angel that radiated with the Glory of God. Waiting for me there was a gathering of people. They divided into three groups; each seemed like a sea of men and women as far as my eyes could see.

The leader of one group was a woman. She stepped forward and embraced me with a hug that was warmer and more genuine than any I had ever experienced. Something about her seemed familiar. She smiled at me with tears in her eyes and thanked me. I apologized for not recognizing her. She explained, "We have never met in person until now."

Her name was Primrose. Born in Zimbabwe, she lost her father by her third birthday. Struggling to survive, she and her mother were desperately praying for help. At age five, she began to receive monthly support through a mission outreach I supported. She was the child to whom my monthly donations provided food, clothes, and education for many years. I received pictures and letters from her throughout the years and prayed for her and her family.

She was exposed to the Gospel through a missions group and received Jesus as her Lord at age eight. After completing college, she went on to medical school, graduating with honors.

Returning to her childhood community, she established a free health clinic. The man she married had accepted Jesus when he heard the Gospel presented by her at a weekly Bible study she led at her office. After giving his life to Christ, he went on to become a pastor. Together they raised six children, served actively in her church, and used the clinic as a platform to share the message about salvation in Jesus.

Primrose turned and pointed to the (what appeared to be millions) people with her that came to know the Savior through her ministry. She said that this would not have been possible without my years of sowing into her life through my financial giving and prayers. I was overwhelmed. Tears of joy flowed from my eyes because I never realized the impact $40 a month would make.

As Primrose backed away, the leader of the next group approached me, and with tears in his eyes, he embraced me as a brother meeting me for the first time. He introduced himself as Jose. Jose shared his story of how his parents planned on aborting him. He was an undesired and unplanned pregnancy of two teenage kids in love but completely unprepared to raise a child. They were counseled at their high school to terminate (fancy language for kill) the pregnancy.

His mother and father were, at the time, two unwed high school students facing a decision that would alter the future of their lives forever. One of their friends told them about a local "pregnancy center" that provided alternatives to abortion. They decided to visit. After weighing both options, his parents decided to keep him. This clinic provided medical care, clothing, food, and counseling.

This pregnancy center was one of the few that established a program to support the father of the children. That's where Jose's dad met me. I had been financially supporting this ministry and volunteering to work with the young men, like his dad. Jose's dad received Jesus after hearing a message I shared with a small group of new fathers.

Jose grew up as the oldest of four children and under the influence of Godly parents. Each year, he spent his summers volunteering at a free Christian camp for underprivileged children.

Jose turned and looked at the myriad of people in his group that came to thank me for sowing financially and spiritually into Jose's Dad and Mom. The seeds I had faithfully planted, through the power of the Holy Spirit, produced a harvest of souls.

The woman leading the third group stepped up and introduced herself as Joy. Her story brought me to my knees. Her parents divorced at a young age, and soon after, her mother remarried. Her stepfather began molesting her when she was seven. The abuse went on for years. At age 15, Joy dropped out of school and ran away from home.

She began working as a dancer in a disreputable establishment to support herself, but soon fell into drug addiction and prostitution. By the time she was 20, she had been arrested 15 times for prostitution and drug possession.

One night, in the depths of despair, she decided to end her life. Wandering the streets, she attempted to work up the courage she needed to overdose on the drugs she had on her. As she was walking past a building, she noticed the door was open. From inside, she could hear a man's voice. An uncontrollable force moved her to get closer. She needed to hear what was being said. This man was sharing his testimony about his journey from a shameful life of addiction to pornography to living in freedom with purpose and passion each day. For the first time, she heard the message of salvation, shared in a simple, honest way that resonated with her.

She went into the building, and standing quietly in the back, she took in the message. At the end, this man appealed to those who listened to invite Jesus to be Lord of their lives. She closed her eyes and invited Jesus in. Instantly, she was flooded with an overwhelming peace she had never experienced. Joy shared that this was the pivotal moment in her life where everything changed.

It took time and support through several Christian ministries for her to get clean and free. Eventually, she married a man she met at her church and had three children. She established a women's ministry for helping women out of sexual abuse, prostitution, alcohol and drug addiction.

Everyone standing behind her was the fruit from the words shared by that man.

Joy stepped a little closer, stared deep into my eyes, making sure I was paying careful attention to what she was about to say. Her words caused my knees to buckle under the weight of God's Mercy. She said, "That man was you!"

When I woke up, all the joy I felt during the dream faded as the reality of my life hit me at once.

Who will I meet in Heaven that was directly IMPACTED by the way I lived my life and leveraged (stewarded) all that was given to me?

You can use this book as a blueprint to build a super-profitable business for decades to come; however, my ultimate objective is to help you become a disciple maker and send your greatest treasure in ahead.

Do not store up for yourselves treasures on earth, where moths and vermin destroy, and where thieves break in and steal. But store up for yourselves treasures in heaven, where moths and vermin do not destroy, and where thieves do not break in and steal. For where your treasure is, there your heart will be also.
Matthew 6:19–21

SPECIAL MESSAGE

THE 800-LBS GORILLA

I'm definitely going to shake a few trees!

OK . . . I know the average adult, male gorilla weighs between 300–400 lbs; however, this sets the context for this book, and it's BIG!

Are you into the "prosperity" or the "poverty" Gospel"? Which is Truth?

Is it about abundant health, wealth, and happiness *or* the belief that material possessions are evil, rich people are ungodly, and self-denial is a means to earn righteousness in God's eyes?

Come on, Dr. Ron (yes, I just referred to myself in the third person), where do you stand?

My answer is always "stewardship." I'm a *stewardship* guy!

Look . . . extremes are always dangerous. Too much emphasis on worldly wealth or, in contrast, a life of scraping by financially is out of balance. There is potential peril when we take scripture out of context to justify our position.

We must seek to discover the original, intended meaning of a given scriptural text through careful, systematic study (exegesis) and find the contemporary relevance of ancient texts, how it relates to us today at all (hermeneutics).

I accepted Jesus as my Lord and Savior 43 years ago at 18 years old. Since then, I have seen a lot. My journey as a believer over the past four-plus decades has exposed me to the many styles of Christian worship, from the very charismatic to the ultraconservative (Orthodox). I have listened to very liberal Christian theology and to extreme fundamentalism. *I have witnessed much variety under the banner of Christ.*

I know there are well-meaning Christians that just get it wrong (on both sides), and there are those who intentionally exploit others, misusing the Word of God for personal gain. I want to be very careful about casting aspersions (OK . . . I had to look up the definition as well. It means *to say harsh, critical things about someone or someone's character*) on brothers and sisters in Christ.

If we stay within *Orthodox Christian doctrine* (away from heresy), there is room for variance. One person believes in the gift of tongues (unknown prayer language) while another believes that gifts like these died with the apostles. I have met those who are for women leading churches and others, vehemently opposed.

This book is about how to build a profitable business that is *Kingdom-Purpose Driven.*

What do I think of the subjects of money, health, relationships, and spirituality as they relate to most Christians?

Whether a person struggles financially, has poor health, experiences bad relationships, or is spiritually weak, the first place I look at is the level of *stewardship* that he or she has exercised in those areas. Whenever I'm questioned about what I mean by *stewardship*, I refer to the Parable of the Talents in Matthew 25:14–30.

Everything (I mean EVERYTHING) is God's. The idea of a self-made man or woman is ridiculous at best. I often challenge people I meet who ascribe to this philosophy by asking them which breath or heartbeat are they responsible for?

There are three main principles from this parable we should pay careful attention to:

1. The Talents (resources) were entrusted to the servants (us) by the Master (God).

2. The servants all received different amounts (resources).

3. Each was expected to bring a reasonable return on investment (ROI) to the Master.

Yes, God is still in the supernatural business; however, my experience tells me, He works on us mostly through the natural.

God is not a genie that we can command, nor an ATM that you program to pour forth abundance just by "doing the right thing." He is a Good Father that loves us and wants to pour out His Blessings on us.

Here's the hard-to-swallow truth for many . . . blessings, many times, come in the form of hardship, pain, trials, illness, and sometimes death (James 1:2). But blessings also may come in our health, wealth, emotional peace, and/or spiritual growth, if we *steward* well what has been given to us in the first place.

Should we, in faith, pray for financial blessings, physical healing, joy, peace, contentment, restoration, or any need we have? YES! All in the Name of Jesus.

God will provide everything we need according to His will, in His timing, and in the fullness He desires. Like the Apostle Paul, let's learn contentment in all circumstances in which we find ourselves in this life (Philippians 4:11–13).

For those of you called to be business owners, my goal is to equip you with the best tools needed to grow your six- or seven-figure business. Unlike many other business training books, my intent is to make sure you stay focused on the purpose for which God has given you a business—to make disciples and glorify His Name. Be the Best Steward and one day hear: "*Well done, good and faithful servant*" (Matthew 25:20–23).

THIS BOOK COMBINES *SPIRITUAL, PRACTICAL, AND PERSONAL* INSTRUCTION ON BUILDING YOUR 7-FIGURE BUSINESS WITH PURPOSE, PASSION, AND PROFIT.

Free Video Training: "What Is Success?" *https://vimeo.com/461351613.*

INTRODUCTION

The way of a fool is right in his own eyes,
but a wise man listens to advice.
Proverbs 12:15 (ESV)

THE BIG PICTURE

It was 4:30 a.m. I had just finished my devotions and Bible study, put on my sneakers, connected my headphones to my iPhone, and headed out for my morning power walk. Social issues had altered many daily routines for most people. Since the gym I worked out at (daily) was closed, I shifted to three daily cardio activities each day, stretching, and some resistance training at home. My early morning walks became my favorite time, when it's dark, quiet, and peaceful.

I always use my workout times to consume audiobooks, sermons, or worship music. This particular morning, I was listening to *Traffic Secrets,* an audiobook by Russell Brunson. I'm a huge fan of Russell and his team at ClickFunnels. This was the second time I was going through this audiobook (yes . . . it's that good). Russell was sharing a story about Garrett White and how ClickFunnels changed everything for his business. White told Russell: "I already had the fire but you (the ClickFunnels software) provided the framework."

Then it hit me!

You know those times when the Holy Spirit ignites something in you and your mind locks in on it, processing and reshaping it into something really powerful?

I immediately stopped walking, pulled my iPhone out of my pocket and captured these ideas in my notes. (I need to document ideas immediately or they'll escape me.) It started as the *fire* and the *framework,* and over the next day, I had another epiphany.

The next morning, during my power walk, I was listening to a teaching series by Dr. Tony Evans. Dr. Evans used a story from the 1986 movie (that I love), *Top Gun,* starring Tom Cruise as Lieutenant Pete "Maverick" Mitchell. I couldn't wait to get back home to my computer and search for scenes of this awesome film. While searching, I came across the trailers for the soon-to-be released *Top Gun 2: Maverick* (some 34 years following the first *Top Gun*). I could feel the adrenaline surge as I watched the F-18 Super Hornets burst with speeds up to 1,190 mph and perform mind-blowing aerial maneuvers with ease. The little boy in me couldn't wait to see this film.

I began to see a direct connection between Russell Brunson's story about the fire and the framework and the F-18 Super Hornet in *Top Gun 2,* except now I saw something new that got me even more excited. Do you ever get that feeling when you know you're onto something so amazing? Well . . . that's exactly what I was experiencing.

The F-18 Super Hornet was obviously made for a purpose—to be a highly specialized weapon capable of offense and defense in times of war or peace. It is one "bad mamma jamma." This was an epiphany moment!

Just think of it, maximum effectiveness for the F-18 can be reached only when three key elements are present, all at the same time. It requires (1) the correct *fuel* to power the jet, (2) a properly constructed and mechanically sound craft (*the framework*), and (3) a pilot adequately trained for peak performance (*the fire*).

This now completed my mission objective. If I am going to facilitate your journey to building your Kingdom-purpose-driven, six- or seven-figure business with massive profit, I would need to include THE *FUEL, THE FRAMEWORK, AND THE FIRE.*

This book is appropriately divided into three sections with purpose.

The FUEL—A Kingdom-Centered Life and Business, "Powered by the Holy Spirit"

The FRAMEWORK—The Seven-Step System to "Maximum Profit"

The FIRE—What You Need to Become "Optimized for Success"

SECTION 1: THE FUEL

Prosperity knits a man to the world. He feels that he is finding his place in it, while really it is finding its place in him.

C.S. Lewis, The Screwtape Letters

1

RED OR BLUE

Trinity softly whispers in his ear, "It's the question that drives you."

Working as a software programmer by day, Thomas Anderson is secretly a computer hacker known as "Neo." He lives alone, barely sleeps, and has no close friends. He spends his nights involved in illegal hacking activities; however, deep inside, he cannot shake the feeling there is something wrong about the world he lives in.

Neo has heard about something called *the Matrix* but doesn't know what it is. *This is the question that has been driving him.*

Neo has been seeking the one known as Morpheus, another hacker, who is believed to have information about the Matrix he has so desperately sought. Through a series of events, Neo is taken to Morpheus in some undisclosed location for a face-to-face meeting that will forever change his life. Morpheus offers Neo a chance to really understand what the Matrix is and how it would change his view of reality forever. He gives him two options.

The red or the blue pill!

Take the blue pill and, he is told, he would return to his everyday life of mediocrity, blinded and enslaved to a powerless life. Or . . . take the red pill and discover a reality that would offer him the opportunity to unlock unimaginable power that lies within him that is accessed only through faith.

This 1999 movie, *The Matrix,* starring Keanu Reeves, Laurence Fishburne, and Carrie-Anne Moss, was not Christian-based; however, it offers some powerful insights to *spiritual warfare.*

The BIG REVEAL: Morpheus shows Neo the reality of his world, then answers the question that drove him to this moment.

Morpheus: "I came to realize the obviousness of the truth. WHAT IS THE MATRIX? . . . CONTROL. The Matrix is a computer-generated dream world, built to keep us under control in order to change a human being into *this.*" (Morpheus holds up a battery.)

Like Neo, you and I once lived in a dream world. We were asleep to the battle going on in the spiritual dimension for our eternal soul. Awakened one day to our real condition, we knew we needed a savior—we needed the grace and love poured out for us at the Cross.

When we accepted Jesus, the Holy Spirit opened our eyes to the war we were in. We discovered that when the Father raised Jesus from the grave, death was defeated, and the devil's fate was sealed (along with all the demons).

It didn't happen right away. Neo needed training to develop his abilities. As his training progressed, so did his confidence. Soon he was able to defeat enemies at every turn.

We, too, must train in order to develop our spiritual strength. As Christians, in order to do effective battle in this world, we must understand that many of the causes originate in the spiritual world and that's where warfare needs to be done. When the manifestation of our earthly problems start in the spiritual realm, we cannot defeat spiritual problems with physical solutions.

We must treat the cause, not the symptom.

Note: I am not dismissing the need for earthly solutions; I am emphasizing the need for daily spiritual battles against the problems we face that originate in the spiritual dimension.

2

TREAT THE CAUSE, NOT THE SYMPTOM

I looked over the email one last time. I clicked on SEND, and suddenly a sense of relief came over me. There had been a severe conflict going on inside me. It was earlier on in my consulting business, and I had only a few clients; however, I knew it was time to fire Ray.

Ray had hired me about six months earlier. In that short period, we became friends, and more importantly, we shared a common faith in Jesus Christ. On the outside, everything looked great. Ray was acting as interim pastor at his church while they were between leadership. Ray was a proud military veteran, loving husband and father. Although his dad started the business, Ray took over when he passed away. The business was going well, and Ray hired me to help scale things up.

During the previous months, a disturbing pattern developed. Ray would miss appointments, and it became more difficult to get him to respond to phone calls, texts, and emails. I had finally reached my breaking point and made the difficult decision to sever our business relationship. Within the next hour, I received a call from Ray. He didn't want to lose me as his coach/consultant and asked me to continue working with him and his team. He apologized for his erratic behavior and promised it wouldn't happen again.

I agreed to continue working with him on one condition: I needed him to honor his commitments to our weekly (virtual) meetings.

For a short time, things seemed to go well, until his behavior began to repeat the old pattern. I quickly confronted him that he was missing appointments and not responding. Then I began to probe deeper. There was no apparent reason for him not showing up for his appointments or not completing his work he committed to. Everything about Ray pointed toward him being a super achiever. He was good looking, in great shape, intelligent, likable, and he loved the Lord.

My years in practice as a doctor taught me to look past the symptoms and unroot the cause. This principle carried over into my consulting/coaching business. What I discovered was shocking.

Ray knew I genuinely cared about him, his family, and his business, and I wanted to see him reach the personal and business success he sought. Before this would happen, I had to discover what the real problem was that kept derailing him.

He finally came clean. He admitted that he battled substance addiction.

I quickly realized that there were deep wounds in his life, going back to childhood that plagued him. All it took was a "trigger," some situation or event that opened the door to use this terrible drug. I would love to tell you that he overcame this addiction quickly, once it was out in the open (to myself, his wife, and an addiction support team), but that was not the case.

I recommended Ray watch a series by Pastor Andy Stanley called *Guardrails* (one of my favorites). Ray's wife and I did our best to encourage Ray to work with us in setting up guardrails to help him stay on track. He resisted for close to two years.

Following several stints in rehab facilities and faithfully attending AA meetings for 100 days straight, he still had setbacks.

Now, here's the key to Ray successfully beating this addiction . . . listen carefully!

The root of the addiction was not in the physical realm; it just manifested there. The root cause was elsewhere and could be defeated only there. He needed a different strategy, a new way of battling this unseen enemy. It was time to armor up!

3

ARMOR UP

Dress for Success is a 1975 book by John T. Molloy about the effect clothing has on a person's success in business and personal life.

In 2016, *Scientific American MIND* published an article "Dress for Success: How Clothes Influence Our Performance." A review by Matthew Hutson and Tori Rodriguez revealed several studies (small studies done in laboratory settings) that suggested that the clothes you wear can affect your mental and physical performance.

Almost 2,000 years earlier, the Apostle Paul, in a letter to the Ephesians (some New Testament scholars advanced the possibility that this letter was meant to be distributed to multiple churches in that area), had something to say about how Christian believers should dress.

This letter can be divided into two parts (chapters 1–3 and 4–6). The first three chapters focused on Christian "doctrine" and the last three chapters on the "duties" of believers. In chapter 6 (the final chapter of his letter), Paul established a clear principle that all Christians (business owners or not) needed to prioritize in life.

If I could share only one piece of advice with any business owner (or any believer), it would be this: YOU WILL DEAL WITH TRIALS/ISSUES throughout your life. In order to be victorious, you must consistently focus on the cause, not the symptoms.

Ephesians 6:12, "For our struggle is not against flesh and blood, but against the rulers, against the authorities, against the powers of this dark world and against the spiritual forces of evil in the heavenly realms."

I love learning from great pastors and teachers like Tony Evans. In his series, *Armor of God* (see *www.tonyevans.org*), Pastor Evans says (paraphrased): "We can't solve spiritual problems with earthly measures." He goes on to emphasize that "We need to deal with the ROOT and not the FRUIT."

Apostle Paul gave us six pieces of "wardrobe" that can equip us for "spiritual victory." Here are some key lessons:

1. Paul tells us to "Put on the full armor of God." It's important to note that God doesn't dress us; that's our responsibility.

2. The purpose is for us to take a stand against the devil's schemes.

3. The first three pieces of armor we are to "put on": the Belt of Truth, the Breastplate of Righteousness, and (our feet fitted with) the Readiness That Comes from the Gospel of Peace.

4. The last three, we are to take up to use when needed. The Shield of Faith, the Helmet of Salvation, and the Sword of the Spirit, which is the Word of God.

Today, Ray is living a victorious life in Christ because he went to war! He waged battle in the spirit realm, accessing the "Full Armor of God." It wasn't until he fully surrendered to the Spirit and stopped trying to win the battle with earthly weapons that he gained VICTORY.

I had the wonderful honor of walking with Ray throughout his journey from being addicted to living his life in the fullness God intends for him. I am no longer his business coach, but we are close brothers in Christ. My wife and I remain very close to Ray and his family.

Like Ray, you and I need to become "Spiritual Warriors," not only doing spiritual battle for ourselves, but for our families, brothers and sisters in Christ, and to those God places in our path.

4

AVOID THIS BIG MISTAKE

OK . . . you might be thinking about all the non-Christian business owners you know that are making or have made fortunes. Many of them are decent citizens; they pay their taxes and are very generous in their giving. *How come they're prospering and I'm not?*

The big mistake here centers around three key issues: Standards, Purpose, and Treasure.

STANDARDS—HOW WE MEASURE PROSPERITY

In 2019, I took my first course by Dr. Frank Turek, "Life's Compass: Jesus, You, and the Essentials of the Faith" (*www.OnlineChristianCourses.school*). Dr. Frank Turek, (Christian apologist, author, speaker, and teacher) points out that there is a truth and a standard that exists that is independent of human standards. This truth or standard is not something we make up; it is something we discover.

In his book, *Stealing from God,* Dr. Turek clearly establishes that God determines what truth is and the standards we are to use to judge good from bad, right from wrong, moral from immoral. We must view the "state" of all people from God's perspective.

God's Word sheds light on our natural state outside the saving Grace of Jesus:

> Romans 3:23 tells us, "for all have sinned and fall short of the glory of God" (CSB).

> 1 Peter 1:15, "But as the one who called you is holy; you also are to be holy in all your conduct" (CSB).

> Ephesians 2:8–9 says, "For you are saved by grace through faith, and this is not from yourselves; it is God's gift—⁹ not from works, so that no one can boast" (CSB).

> Matthew 16:26, "For what will it benefit someone if he gains the whole world yet loses his life? Or what will anyone give in exchange for his life?" (CSB).

I'm convinced that most who read this book and implement the steps can build a profitable business.

WE MUST MEASURE ALL THINGS BY GOD'S STANDARDS.

Focus on building your relationship with God and steward well all He has given you with a heart of thanksgiving.

Winston Churchill said, "We make a living by what we get. We make a life by what we give."

PURPOSE

God creates each person with a purpose that only they can fulfill. In order to operate in that calling, we must be submitted to the Lordship of Jesus. When we are saved by faith in Jesus, we now have specific assignments all aimed at making disciples by the fruit we bear. That fruit should show up in every facet of our personal and professional lives.

Matthew 28:19–20, "Go, therefore, and make disciples of all nations, baptizing them in the name of the Father and of the Son and of the Holy Spirit, teaching them to observe everything I have commanded you. And remember, I am with you always, to the end of the age" (CSB).

Many men and women who have attained tremendous wealth in this life will spend an eternity separated from their Creator because they refused to accept Jesus as Lord.

TREASURE

The Gospel is the "Great Equalizer." No matter your place of birth, ethnicity, gender, physical appearance, or financial status, you can accumulate incredible wealth.

My wife, Johanna, and I launched ROAR, a community for Christian Business Owners that have already built successful businesses. Our vision is to inspire, empower, and equip these men and women to use the platform of business to fulfill the "Great Commission" and be disciple makers (Matthew 28:19–20).

I can speak with boldness into the lives of these successful entrepreneurs about being better stewards because I spent many years (as a believer) growing my businesses and worldly wealth with little-to-no focus on the purpose that was given to me.

In Matthew 6:19–21, Jesus says, "Don't store up for yourselves treasure] on earth, where moths and rust destroy and where thieves break in and steal. But store up for yourselves treasures in heaven, where neither moth nor rust destroys, and where thieves don't break in and steal. For where your treasure is, there your heart will be also" (CSB).

This principle levels the playing field for every Christian, no matter their earthly status. Any believer, through faithfulness and obedience, can send their treasure ahead! Kingdom economics and wealth accumulation operate quite differently than our earthly system.

The mindset of the Christian Business Owner is different from all others. We function in Kingdom economics by:

- Operating our lives and businesses by God's *Standards*, not the world's standards.

- Seeking to fulfill the specific *purpose* God has for us.

- Focusing more on storing up *treasures* in Heaven than on Earth.

- *Stewarding* well whatever God Blesses us here in this life.

5

STAY FUELED UP WITH THESE SEVEN SPIRITUAL DISCIPLINES

1. WORSHIP

We were made to worship our God.

The call to worship is found in God's Word from Genesis to Revelation. Worshiping our Lord is our response to how great He is. Making worship a daily practice ushers us into the presence of our King.

Here are just a few passages of scripture related to this subject:

- Psalm 99:5, "Exalt the Lord our God; worship at his footstool! Holy is he!" (ESV).

- Hebrews 12:28, "Therefore let us be grateful for receiving a kingdom that cannot be shaken, and thus let us offer to God acceptable worship, with reverence and awe" (ESV).

- Luke 4:8, "And Jesus answered him, 'It is written, 'You shall worship the Lord your God, and him only shall you serve'" (ESV).

- Isaiah 12:5, "Sing praises to the Lord, for he has done gloriously; let this be made known in all the earth" (ESV).

- Romans 12:1–2, "I appeal to you therefore, brothers, by the mercies of God, to present your bodies as a living sacrifice, holy and acceptable to God, which is your spiritual worship. Do not be conformed to this world, but be transformed by the renewal of your mind, that by testing you may discern what is the will of God, what is good and acceptable and perfect" (ESV).

2. PRAYER

Daily communication with our Heavenly Father. When we pray, we bring our needs and the needs of others before Him. I can think of no greater example for our need to pray often than Jesus.

- Philippians 4:6, "Do not be anxious about anything, but in everything by prayer and supplication with thanksgiving let your requests be made known to God" (ESV).

- 1 Thessalonians 5:17, "Pray without ceasing" (ESV).

- James 5:16, "Therefore, confess your sins to one another and pray for one another, that you may be healed. The prayer of a righteous person has great power as it is working" (ESV).

- Ephesians 6:18, "Praying at all times in the Spirit, with all prayer and supplication. To that end keep alert with all perseverance, making supplication for all the saints" (ESV).

3. STUDY

God's Word is our blueprint for life. It's impossible to obey God's Word if we don't know it. Getting into God's Word is the first step of His Word getting into us!

- Acts 17:11, "Now these Jews were more noble than those in Thessalonica; they received the word with all eagerness, examining the Scriptures daily to see if these things were so" (ESV).

- 2 Timothy 3:16, "All Scripture is God-breathed and is useful for teaching, rebuking, correcting, and training in righteousness" (ESV).

- 1 Peter 3:15, "But in your hearts honor Christ the Lord as holy, always being prepared to make a defense to anyone who asks you for a reason for the hope that is in you; yet do it with gentleness and respect" (ESV).

4. FELLOWSHIP

We are made to be in community. Have you ever heard the phrase, "We are better together"? The Scripture clearly directs us to stay deeply connected.

- Hebrews 10:25, " . . . not neglecting to meet together, as is the habit of some, but encouraging one another, and all the more as you see the Day drawing near" (ESV).

- Proverbs 27:17, "Iron sharpens iron, and one man sharpens another" (ESV).

- Acts 2:42, "And they devoted themselves to the apostles' teaching and the fellowship, to the breaking of bread and the prayers" (ESV).

- Ephesians 5:19, "Addressing one another in psalms and hymns and spiritual songs, singing and making melody to the Lord with your heart" (ESV).

5. FASTING

Denying the flesh for a time to devote our efforts to seeking God in prayer.

- Acts 14:23, "And when they had appointed elders for them in every church, with prayer and fasting they committed them to the Lord in whom they had believed" (ESV).

- Acts 13:2–3, "While they were worshiping the Lord and fasting, the Holy Spirit said, 'Set apart for me Barnabas and Saul for the work to which I have called them.' Then after fasting and praying they laid their hands on them and sent them off" (ESV).

- Matthew 6:18, "That your fasting may not be seen by others but by your Father who is in secret. And your Father who sees in secret will reward you" (ESV).

- 2 Chronicles 20:2–4, "Some men came and told Jehoshaphat, 'A great multitude is coming against you from Edom, from beyond the sea; and, behold, they are in Hazazon-tamar' (that is, Engedi). Then Jehoshaphat was afraid and set his face to seek the Lord, and proclaimed a fast throughout all Judah. And Judah assembled to seek help from the Lord; from all the cities of Judah they came to seek the Lord" (ESV).

- Esther 4:16, "Go, gather all the Jews to be found in Susa, and hold a fast on my behalf, and do not eat or drink for three days, night or day. I and my young women will also fast as you do" (ESV).

- Nehemiah 1:4, "As soon as I heard these words I sat down and wept and mourned for days, and I continued fasting and praying before the God of heaven" (ESV).

6. MEDITATION

Deep contemplation on the truths of God. Many Christians avoid meditation because they associate it with Eastern religious practices. There is a clear difference between Eastern meditation and Christian meditation. Eastern disciplines involve emptying oneself while the Christian discipline of meditation is about being filled by God's Holy Presence.

- Joshua 1:8, "This Book of the Law shall not depart from your mouth, but you shall meditate on it day and night, so that you may be careful to do according to all that is written in it. For then you will make your way prosperous, and then you will have good success" (ESV).

- Psalm 19:14, "Let the words of my mouth and the meditation of my heart be acceptable in your sight, O Lord, my rock and my redeemer" (ESV).

- Psalm 1:2, "But his delight is in the law of the Lord, and on his law he meditates day and night" (ESV).

- Philippians 4:8, "Finally, brothers, whatever is true, whatever is honorable, whatever is just, whatever is pure, whatever is lovely, whatever is commendable, if there is any excellence, if there is anything worthy of praise, think about these things" (ESV).

7. WITNESSING

Sharing the Gospel with others. Being an effective witness involves how we live before others as well as what, how, and when we share our faith.

- Mathew 28:18–20, "And Jesus came and said to them, 'All authority in heaven and on earth has been given to me. Go therefore and make disciples of all nations, baptizing them in[a] the name of the Father and of the Son and of the Holy Spirit, teaching them to observe all that I have commanded you. And behold, I am with you always, to the end of the age'" (ESV).

- Acts 1:8, "But you will receive power when the Holy Spirit has come upon you, and you will be my witnesses in Jerusalem and in all Judea and Samaria, and to the end of the earth" (ESV).

Free Video Training: "The Truth about Money," *https://vimeo.com/461347699*.

UNSTOPPABLE SUMMARY OF THE FUEL

- We will face all sorts of trials in business and life.
- We are in a real battle that we cannot see with our eyes. It is a spiritual war, and we are called to fight.
- We must put on the Full Armor of God" for daily spiritual warfare.
- We cannot solve a spiritual problem with earthly solutions.
- We must stay Kingdom-focused.
- We must develop the regular practice of the Seven Spiritual Disciplines.

Now . . . back to our F-18 Super Hornet analogy. We're on the deck of the aircraft carrier all *fueled* up (with the Holy Spirit). It's time to make sure all the necessary parts are in place and functioning properly. We can't take off until we know the *framework* is right.

SECTION 2:
THE FRAMEWORK

*Great Businesses are built on solid
foundations by extraordinary leaders.*

6

BUILD YOUR BUSINESS ON A
ROCK-SOLID FOUNDATION

In 2018, I was hired by Specialized Trust Company, a self-directed investment company to help them build out a system for operating their business that would allow for consistency and scalability. Since I was already a client of this company, I was familiar with their products. In order to be most effective, I had to empty all my preconceived ideas and knowledge of their business and start from scratch.

I first interviewed the owners, then all their team. I wanted to see the company from each of their perspectives. I also wanted to know what function they thought they served and its importance to the vitality of the company. I had to assess the current company culture and the type and level of leadership.

My first objective was to spend time with the two partners that founded the company and continue to work in the business. I needed to know their objectives, dreams, and vision, not only for the company but also for themselves. I wanted them to get CLEAR first about what they *really wanted.*

In my experience, most business owners make huge, fundamental mistakes that cost them emotionally, financially, and even physically (unneeded stress).

Before a skyscraper can successfully be built, there must be a solid foundation laid.

In Matthew 7: 24–27, Jesus uses the foundation of a house (built on rock or sand) as an analogy for those listening to be hearers and doers of His Word:

> "Everyone then who hears these words of mine and does them will be like a wise man who built his house on the rock. And the rain fell, and the floods came, and the winds blew and beat on that house, but it did not fall, because it had been founded on the rock. And everyone who hears these words of mine and does not do them will be like a foolish man who built his house on the sand.[27] And the rain fell, and the floods came, and the winds blew and beat against that house, and it fell, and great was the fall of it" (ESV).

In 2019, I had the honor of meeting and speaking to Michael and Luz Gerber. Michael is the author of the best-selling books, *The E-Myth* and *The E-Myth Revisited*. Michael and I spent some time discussing the common mistakes business owners make.

The "E-Myth" stands for the Entrepreneurial Myth. Simply restated, the skill of doing something is NOT THE SAME SKILL required to run a business doing that skill. Running a business requires specialized knowledge of business structure, leadership, culture building, systems, and processes. (You probably need to read that more than once.)

Back to Specialized Trust Company.

The owners had worked hard to build a good company; however, they knew to build a great company that would allow them to scale and reach their goals in business and life, they needed more. We spent the year building out and implementing my Seven-Step System into their business in order to scale.

Using my Seven-Step System, I've been able to help solopreneurs, entrepreneurs, and small- to medium-sized businesses ($1M–$100M).

I'm going to lay out my Seven-Step System, which is influenced by a vast number of sources from my more than 37 years in business (to date).

7

MY SEVEN-STEP SYSTEM

STEP 1: Build a Better You . . . Build a Better Business

STEP 2: Establish a Proven Business Operating System

STEP 3: Create Your "Unfair Marketing Advantage"

STEP 4: Craft an Extraordinary Experience

STEP 5: Build an Inspired Culture

STEP 6: Lead by Design

STEP 7: Growth through Accountability

STEP 1—BUILD A BETTER YOU . . . BUILD A BETTER BUSINESS

I was speaking to a group of 200+ business owners. I asked them, "Who remembers being in grade school, middle school, and high school?" I then told them how I made the top half of my class . . . *POSSIBLE!!!* (Someone had to be in the bottom of the class to make it possible for those at the top.)

I have received so much feedback in the past decade from business owners who felt more empowered after hearing my story. The vast majority of entrepreneurs I've met have experienced personal struggles early on in life, and oftentimes, carry some self-limiting habits and beliefs into their adulthood, which impacts their business growth.

Maybe you can relate?

Nineteen years of academic struggles took a sudden change after my freshman year of college.

I finished my first year at Rutgers (College of Arts and Sciences in Camden, New Jersey) in 1977 with under a 2.0 GPA (Yikes). That summer, I worked for a roofing company driving trucks. My boss asked me to shift from driving trucks to working on one of the roofing crews. (It was a big increase in pay.) Joe was the foreman I was assigned to work under, and little did I know, but God would use him to change the course of my life.

It was difficult to see at the time; however, looking back on my life, I see God's handiwork continually working to mold my destiny. It seemed to me (at that time) that Joe lived solely to make my time at work as miserable as possible. He took every opportunity to scream at me and degrade me in front of all the other roofers.

Note: If you're in a place right now where you can't see how God is working through your circumstances, just stand firm (Ephesians 6:13). God's promises are 100 percent reliable. He is working to refine you, bring out your best, and produce endurance that leads to a greater character (James 1:1–4).

One afternoon during our lunch break, I was sitting with Mike, one of my best friends, who had led me to the Lord about a year earlier. Mike and all the other roofers were part of the union (I was the only nonunion worker on the crew). Joe had no leverage over them, so he chose to take out all his frustrations in life on me. Mike witnessed Joe's cruelty to me and realized I was boiling mad.

I told Mike that when I got back from lunch, I planned on doing serious harm to Joe. In my mind, I had it all planned out; this would be the last day Joe would ever abuse me (or anyone else). By God's amazing grace, Mike, with great sympathy and kindness, calmed me down by reminding me of God's greater purpose for my life and that doing harm to Joe wasn't part of it.

Later that afternoon during a break, we were all sitting around together. I was reading a book to help me get a head start on the next semester. Joe couldn't pass on the opportunity to put me down in front of the entire crew. This time I didn't remain silent.

I'd had enough. I shouted at Joe that he was a loser and how I was going to finish college, become very successful, and then come back and buy this company so I could fire him. (I can't fully remember the exact words, but I believe there may have been a few cuss words woven in.)

At that moment, something inside me changed! I was convinced I couldn't spend the rest of my life working for men (or women) like Joe. I was focused on changing my future.

When I returned to college that fall (Ocean County Community), I was determined to reverse the academic trend I had settled for in my past. I knew that I was a slow reader and that my reading comprehension was low, so I simply doubled my effort. If one of my peers had to study one hour to get an A on the test, I studied two. What happened surprised me at first. I started getting As and Bs. Each success gave me more confidence and determination to succeed.

I've come to realize that through my earlier education inadequacies, I had allowed my "learning challenges" to limit my belief in my potential. It wasn't until I was motivated sufficiently (thanks to Joe) that I pushed through my self-imposed limits and realized my potential. It's been more than four decades since that pivotal point in my life. Looking back, I see the effects of compounding. The more I achieved, the more I was capable of achieving. At 19, my lifelong study of success began.

It first started with the selfish objective of how I could be more successful, but over time, evolved into an insatiable drive to help others, like you, to achieve everything in life you were created for. God can use the "Joes" in your life as a means for powerful change. Trauma, pain, and suffering can be the catalyst for major growth.

It takes faith to step into the destiny God has for you. Building a profitable, God-centered business can change many lives, other than your own.

I spend three to four hours a day learning and studying. I have learned from great teachers, books, seminars, online courses, and private mentors; however, the greatest advances in my life and business came from application of what I learned. My failures in many ways taught me the most.

There are three things that impact your ability to succeed:

1. God's will

2. Your DNA

3. Your Lifestyle/Behaviors

1. God's Will: What God Says about You

- You are fearfully and wonderfully made (Psalm 139:14).

- God made you in His own image (Genesis 1:27).

- He knew you before you were conceived (Jeremiah 1:5).

- You were created for good works (Ephesians 2:1).

God's Word reveals His purpose for our life and our great worth to Him. He has plans to use us for His Glory, but *we must choose to accept the mission.*

Free Video Training: "The Power of Your Story," *https://vimeo.com/461360039.*

In 2014, I was part of a business mastermind. There were about 30 bright entrepreneurs in the room with the purpose of seeing how we could help each other.

We would each have a certain amount of time to be "hot seated." This was our time to stand in front of the group to tell them what our business is and where we need help. The group would then offer advice, key resources, and direction.

There were only two to three in that group that were followers of Jesus. I was friends with everyone in attendance, and they all knew me. I began with asking them a favor: If they were to see a specific niche where I should be focusing my speaking and consulting, please point it out. Within five minutes, one man raised his hand and proclaimed that I should focus my business in the Christian community. The entire group instantly joined him in full (enthusiastic) agreement.

My response was instantaneous. I told them that I had contemplated this direction before but felt I needed to take a wider approach and not limit my expertise and abilities to just Christians.

In hindsight, God was clearly speaking through this group (mostly unbelievers) directly to me, and I dismissed the call.

Despite my failure to hear His voice and obey, God was patient with me. He continued speaking to me through others and His precious word, until I listened. I don't remember the date, but I clearly remember the experience.

During my prayer time, I heard (inside my mind) God challenge me. I had been telling God for a while, "Here I am God, Send Me" (from Isaiah 6:8). God quietly reminded me of these words and asked If I meant it.

I accepted the call!

If you have any doubts about how valuable you are to God, read and meditate on His Word, spend time with Him in prayer, and reject the lies of the enemy.

2. Your DNA

Called the *blueprint of life*, DNA is the chemical name for the molecule that carries genetic instructions in all living things.

- DNA contains all the information needed to build your body. Your unique combination of DNA determines things such as your eye color, hair color, height, and even the size of your nose. The DNA in your cells is responsible for these physical attributes as well as many others.

- Human DNA comes in 23 pairs of packages called chromosomes. These chromosomes are large bundles of tightly packed DNA. Your mother and father each donated 23 chromosomes, which paired up to give you your full set of 23.

- The information (data) stored in a single cell is about 1.5 gigabytes, and about 150 zettabytes (150×10^{21}) in the entire body. We are fearfully and wonderfully made indeed (Psalm 139:14).

- You had no choice in determining your DNA . . . God chose for you. Don't focus on your DNA, rather, focus on what you can do to *influence its expression (epigenetics)*.

3. Your Lifestyle/Behaviors

Reaching heights of more than 300 feet, the tallest tree on Earth is the redwood. There are about 50 living along the Pacific Coast that measure at least 360 feet. Certain redwoods today are greater than 2,000 years old. Despite being the tallest of trees, the redwood seed is about the same size as a tomato seed (easily fitting on the tip of your finger).

What's even more amazing is the fact that all the DNA necessary to direct the construction of each of these magnificent trees is completely contained in the tiny seed, holding the potential to build a 300-foot tree with roots that go down 6–12 feet and grow to 50-foot-wide and live longer than 1,000 years.

I hope you caught the word *potential* in the above paragraph. The ability for these trees to reach their full size and have a high quality of health is dependent on the environment they're in, with variables affecting them like weather, soil nutrition, and protection against external damage (infection, intense fire, and humans).

Your DNA code is fixed at conception; however, it can be affected by your lifestyle and your environment.

Epigenetics—You are more than your genetics.

- Epigenetics: The study of changes in organisms caused by modification of gene expression rather than alteration of the genetic code itself. *Your age, disease state, environment, and lifestyle all have an impact on the switching on and off of genes.*

- Why is this important? While you can't change your age or DNA, you can change your environment and lifestyle, which can have a positive effect on your health, vitality, and longevity.

Consider these passages: Science today continues to reveal the truth in Scripture.

- Daniel 1:11–16, "Daniel, Shadrach, Meshach, and Abednego ate vegetables and drank water."

- Proverbs 14:30, "A heart at peace gives life to the body, but envy rots the bones" (NIV).

- Proverbs 3:7–8, "Be not wise in your own eyes; fear the LORD AND turn away from evil. It will be healing to your flesh and refreshment to your bones" (ESV).

- Proverbs 17:22, "A joyful heart is good medicine, but a crushed spirit dries up the bones" (ESV).

Our success in life is directed by God's Will for us and impacted by the combination of our DNA and lifestyle choices.

One of my favorite statements is "stack the deck in your favor." Doing the wise and prudent thing isn't always a guarantee for successful outcomes but it does shift the potential in our favor.

God is Sovereign and always has our best in mind. His ways are better than ours (Isaiah 55:8–10), and we need to trust Him (Proverbs 3:5–6). With this in mind, let's take a look at our responsibility.

God gives us a "free will" to choose the following:

- To reject or accept salvation offered through the atoning sacrifice of Jesus

- How much spiritual growth and maturity we'll pursue

- Our degree of stewardship over our finances

- The level of care we exercise over our health—diet, exercise, rest, safety

- To focus to build strong, loving, Christ-centered marriages

- Whether to surround ourselves with Godly fellowship

- How often we look for opportunities to share the Gospel with others

- Will we commit to developing the gifts God placed in us to impact the world for Him

If you're paying careful attention, you'll see the main point—you and I have a responsibility to be active players in the life God has blessed us with. Our responsibility is limited to the things we've been given control of.

God's Word is the main source for decision-making. Whether it gives us direction, directly or indirectly, we should be seeking guidance through the Holy Spirit.

When we make the right choices and create empowering habits, spiritually, physically, relationally, and financially, we *stack the deck* in our favor toward better results.

UNSTOPPABLE SUMMARY: BUILD A BETTER YOU, BUILD A BETTER BUSINESS

You were born with a unique combination of DNA.
You are "one of a kind"!

Your journey in life molds, shapes, prepares, and equips you for a purpose only you can fulfill.

God's favor is toward you. He has created you for His Glory and to complete a mission only you can.

If you want to build a better business, consider the wisdom in building a better you . . .
Mind, Body, and Spirit.

You were born to win, but to be a winner, you must plan to win, prepare to win, and expect to win.
Zig Ziglar

Once you're dialed in to building a better you, it's time to establish a business operating system that improves efficiency, reduces unnecessary problems, and maximizes profitability.

STEP 2—ESTABLISH A PROVEN BUSINESS OPERATING SYSTEM

Success leaves clues!

My guess is that this is a saying you've heard, but did you ever stop to think deeply about what that means?

Astronomers, research scientists, historians, theologians, philosophers, archeologists, economists, politicians, market analysts, and meteorologists, to name just a few, all look for *patterns* in their respective fields.

Patterns are built into the very fabric of God's creation. They help us determine predictability. Having a *proven* business system can help you break through to that next level or send your business vertical!

When I work with the company leadership, I first establish what systems they already have in place and how effective those systems are. The next step is to use the system below to fill in the gaps, strengthen weaker systems, and eliminate what doesn't work.

Each company's needs are slightly different and require getting a clear picture of the nature of the business, the goals and dreams of the owners, the elements needed and the priority of those elements.

Let's start with the basics.

What Is a Business System?

- A system is a procedure, process, method, or course of action designed to achieve a specific result.

- Its component parts and interrelated steps work together for the good of the whole.

- *Creating effective business systems is the only way to attain results that are consistent, measurable, and ultimately benefit customers. There are 9 Key Components.*

I have identified *9 Key Components* of a solid business system that should serve most entrepreneurs:

- your vision, mission, strategy, and tactics

- your 1-year plan

- core values

- your team

- scorecards

- problem solving

- the process

- identifying opportunities and threats

- building and maintaining growth

1. Vision, Mission, Strategy, and Tactics

I needed a name for it!

I was in the gym, working up a good sweat on the *elliptical* machine, watching the Animal Planet Channel. I got hooked on a series they did on the "Big Cats of Africa." One morning, I was watching an episode on lions and lionesses. They were discussing how they used their roar as a way of communicating.

A part of my brain went into overdrive once they revealed this amazing fact!

Male lions are very territorial. Their domain typically covers about two square miles. With their keen sense of hearing and their familiarity with the roars of their pride members, they are able to detect the roar of another male invading their area. They roar loudly as a warning to tell the "enemy" to stay out, declaring their dominion over their territory.

That was it! We would name our community ROAR as a metaphor. We are challenging Christian Business Owners to *take back the territory God has given to them.* We have lost vital territory because of our sin or because we yielded it to the enemy (the devil). This includes marriages, families, business, ministries, and influence.

ROAR is a community for Christian Business Owners. Johanna (my wife) and I were led to create ROAR in early 2017. God placed a burden in us to call those who had built a successful business, and now it was time to focus on the ultimate purpose for that business.

Many Christians have built strong businesses, often at the expense of their marriages, health, and more importantly, their spiritual maturity. Too much compromise and not enough stewardship of what God has blessed them with.

Without judgment, and with deep conviction, I can speak with great authority here because *I was that person for decades.* One foot in the world and one in the Kingdom. I spent most of my time focusing on building financial wealth at the cost of the more important things.

Can you relate?

Perhaps you're in that season of life where you're growing your business and you've fallen into this trap of "priority challenges." Your drive for financial success outpaces all other drives to serve God.

STOP right where you are, confess to the Father your struggle, and ask for the Holy Spirit to enable you to shift to daily seeking God's direction and will. He can put you back on track, helping fulfill the plan He has for you. *Seek Him First!* Matthew 6:33, "But seek first the kingdom of God and his righteousness, and all these things will be provided for you" (CSB).

Note: I'll use ROAR (our private community of Christian Business Owners) as a real-life example, wherever I can, to help you understand the principle.

Vision (5–20 Years)—WHY YOU DO WHAT YOU DO—Defines where you see your business/company in the future:

- It describes your hopes and dreams.

- It tells of your impact on the greater good.

- You communicate who and what you're inspiring to change.

Cameron Herold, in his book, *Double Double*, describes how to create a "Vivid Vision." You document a bolder and more detailed picture of how your business is creating a larger impact, including accomplishments that are well recognized inside and outside your niche. (For more, I would encourage you to get a copy to read or the audiobook.)

Our *Vivid Vision* for ROAR: A community of 100,000 (plus) Christian Business Owners living all out for the sake of the Gospel. Millions will be led to a saving relationship with Jesus. We will help lead a revolution in the marketplace that will change the standard of how business is done and how employees (the team) are cared for.

Simon Sinek, in his book, *The Infinite Game*, suggests building a business around what he labels a "Just Cause" (the WHY). This allows you to attract and keep team members that buy into that WHY. He notes that the *just cause* of your company is what creates the internal drive of every contributing team member and results in profit.

What's your just cause? How will you convey that message to your team and the marketplace?

Profit follows your vision, not the other way around!

Mission (1–5 Years)—WHAT YOU DO—Defines why you exist and why it's important. It also tells how you'll achieve your Vision:

- What do you do?

- What value do you bring?

- What problems do you solve with your products or services?

- Whom do you serve, and how do you serve them?

- Outline your desired outcomes, goals, or achievements

Strategy (weekly, 1 Year)—HOW YOU DO IT—Defines the process (long- and short-term goals) on how the Mission and Vision will be fulfilled.

- What resources are needed?

- How should resources be prioritized?

- What systems will be followed?

- Whom do you need?

- How should benchmarks and metrics be identified?

Tactics—The specific actions taken within your strategy.

- Strategy is broken down into the individual steps.

- Concrete actions that are clearly documented and identify who is responsible, what resources are needed, and a timeline for completion.

- Must be flexible and easily altered to adapt to changing circumstances.

EXAMPLE

ROAR

Vision: Our Vision is to impact the world by fulfilling the great commission in Matthew 28:19 through Christians using their business platform, first, to make disciples, then profit.

Mission: Our Mission is to Inspire, Empower, and Equip 1 Million Christian Business Owners to leverage their influence to make disciples in their marketplace, home, church, community, and nation.

Strategy: Our strategy is to establish a minimum of two ROAR communities (60 members each) in every state in the United States, then expand worldwide.

Tactics: We meet four times yearly for two days. Weekly virtual training provided for all members. Separate weekly Men and Women meetings (virtual) for prayer and support. Provide business coaching programs to help Christian Business Owners thrive in the marketplace.

Check ROAR, *www.roarevent.com*

ACTION STEPS

1. Gather together your leadership team (if you have one).

2. Write out your Vivid Vision—no more than one page.

3. Determine your Mission.

4. Establish your Strategy to achieve your Mission.

5. Settle on the tactics will you use for accomplishing your strategy.

6. Create a *living* document for all to see.

7. Have a team meeting to reveal your *Vivid Vision, Mission, Strategy, and Tactics.*

2. 1-Year Plan

I used to recommend writing a plan to lay out your one-, three-, and ten-year goals. This is no longer my advice due to the rapidly changing world we live in today. I believe it is better, once you have your Vision (5–10 years out), to create a 1-Year Plan.

Events outside of your control may require you to act quickly, to shift and refocus your strategy. Your *1-Year Plan* allows you to pivot and refocus when conditions affecting your business shift. *The strength of your business will be directly related to your ability to quickly adjust your tactics and strategies as necessary.*

SIX STEPS TO CREATING YOUR 1-YEAR PLAN

1. Assemble your key team members

2. Schedule one to three hours

3. Establish your target gross annual revenue and profit

4. Identify your key metrics (measures)

    - number of units sold or number of new clients

    - what resources will be needed

    - who will be needed (additional help)

    - what key strategic partners are needed

5. The outcome of this meeting is to have three to seven items that take the highest priority for the year. They need to be

    - specific

    - measurable

    - attainable

6. Be flexible when needed to make quick, well thought-out shifts.

EXAMPLE

ROAR 1-YEAR PLAN

- Our 2020 goal is to max out our community to 60 active members.

- Establish strong accountability and community through weekly virtual meetings for men and twice per month virtual meetings for women (Lionesses).

- Provide 12 (once per month) business training calls.

- Provide six relationship workshops (virtual).

- Meet together for fellowship once per quarter.

- Four two-day ROAR events.

- Exceed everyone's expectations.

Your 1-Year Plan is the most important part of driving your company forward. It's the vehicle that moves you toward your Vision, one year at a time. Your team members may have a more difficult time seeing themselves with you three, five, or even ten years down the road; however, they can easily picture being with you over the next year.

ACTION STEPS

1. Gather your leadership team.

2. Determine where you want your company to be one year from now.

3. What three to five major items (ROCKS) need to happen to get you there?

4. What KPIs (key performance indicators) will measure your success?

5. What resources will you require to make this happen?

6. Document your plan and distribute to your entire team.

3. Core Values

Definition: The set of vital, non-negotiable, guiding principles for your business/company. These become the filter through which all decisions are made. (Recommended to establish three to seven.)

Application: These are used in *hiring, firing, rewarding,* and *promoting.* Your culture is built around them.

SEVEN STEPS TO CREATING YOUR CORE VALUES

1. Assemble key team members (solopreneurs might recruit a few close business professionals that they respect to aid them).

2. Each person identifies two to three icons (influencers in your industry/field) that, if cloned, would take your company to the top.

3. Identify the characteristics these people engender.

4. Create a written list of these characteristics and discuss them.

5. Begin a robust discussion of each one and begin the elimination process.

6. Narrow the list to the three to seven that are absolutely necessary values that resonate with everyone.

7. Company core values typically don't change. They may need to be modified over time to better fit and drive the culture.

ROAR CORE VALUES

- The Bible is Our Authority and Standard We Operate Through (2 Timothy 3:16, CSB).

- The First Purpose of Business is Making Disciples, the Second is Profit (Matthew 28:19–20, CSB).

- The Holy Spirit Leads, We Follow in Obedience (Romans 8:14, CSB).

- We Honor, Respect, Support, and Love Each Other (Romans 12:10, CSB).

- We are Committed to Good Stewardship of All We are Blessed With (Matthew 14:30, CSB).

- We battle spiritual problems with spiritual warfare. We put on the "Full Armor of God" (Ephesians 6:10–20, CSB).

- We take on the position of leadership in our homes, businesses, friendships, churches, and communities (Hebrews 13:7, CSB).

ACTION STEPS

1. Spend time listing all your personal core values.

2. Which of your core values need to be your company's core values?

3. Gather your team together. Don't reveal your list of company core values until later.

4.   Have each team member make a list of what they think the company's core values should be.

5.   Compile a list (on a chart or white board) of everyone's chosen core values.

6.   Through discussion, narrow the list to your top four to seven.

7.   Write a short description that accurately expresses each core value.

8.   Create a document for everyone to see.

9.   You use this document to hire, fire, promote, and reward all team members.

10. Review these regularly. You may discover the need to add, subtract, or amend in the first year. Once you feel that they completely represent your company, they become your guide through which every business decision must pass.

4. Your Team

Hiring the right people is critical to your company's overall health and success. Here are some guidelines to help you:

•   Do they buy into your company vision and mission?

•   Would they be a good fit for your Company Core Values?

•   Do they have the skills (capacity) necessary to do the job?

•   Are they willing (and excited) to do what's necessary in that role?

Whether you're a solopreneur or have many team members (I don't like the term *employees*) in your company, you should have an organizational chart.

You may occupy many or all of the roles now; however, if you plan on growing, you'll need to give yourself regular promotions. Here's what I mean: As your income and profit expand, you'll hire people to do jobs that are not in alignment with your core strengths or reflect the highest and best use of time, talent, money, and skill set.

Having an organizational chart is a clear way of visualizing all the moving parts of your business and who is responsible.

YOUR ORGANIZATIONAL CHART

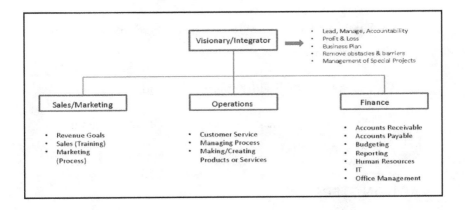

ACTION STEPS

1. Build your company organizational chart with placeholders for all positions.

2. Put the name in each position of who occupies that role. (If you're a solopreneur, small business, or just getting started, you might occupy most if not all positions.)

3. Consider outsourcing team members.

4. Post this organizational chart where you and your leadership team can see it.

5. Scorecards

What gets measured and watched, improves.

Some measurement of performance, achievement, or activity that is quantifiable, objective, and clearly understood. Other names include Key Performance Indicators (KPIs), Dashboard, or Measurables.

- Keeping score tells you if you're winning.

- They remove subjectivity and allow any for accountability.

- Everyone has a number to help them measure their performance.

- They can create healthy competition and/or teamwork.

- Help identify where you are off track, so problems are more quickly resolved.

ACTION STEPS

1. Everyone must have a scorecard so they know (measure) their performance.

2. Determine measures that are clear for each position. If you have competent people in those positions, consider getting their input.

3. Once their metrics are established, ensure that each team member is clear on what is expected of them.

4. Use these scorecards to find ways to give positive feedback when they meet or exceed their goals. *Reward the behavior you want repeated.*

6. Problem Solving

You can't fix what you can't identify.

Early on in my chiropractic practice, a patient was referred to me by some friends. Mr. Lewis (not his real name) was in his 70s and was a retired *shop teacher*. He spent much of his day as a volunteer at the local Boys and Girls Club.

I had all my patients complete detailed questionnaires about their health history and their chief complaint(s). Afterwards, I would perform a thorough consultation and examination before determining if any other tests were necessary.

Mr. Lewis's chief complaint was back pain. He also had a chiropractic treatment in his past. During my physical exam, I noticed three small dots tattooed on his lower back in a triangle pattern. When I questioned him about these dots, he told me he had been treated in the past for prostate cancer, which included surgery and radiation treatment (the reason for the three dot tattoos).

Now, here's the catch. On his intake paperwork, in the section on past surgeries or other relevant conditions, he never mentioned his prostate cancer, surgery, or radiation!

When asked why . . . he told me, "I forgot."

I wondered how in the world you could forget to mention you had been diagnosed and treated for cancer. After taking some low-back X-rays, I discovered a collapsed lumbar vertebra. His back pain was from cancer that had spread from his prostate. He was the first patient I lost due to cancer.

Had I treated Mr. Lewis for mechanical back pain, I would have provided no real relief and I would have delayed critical treatment he needed from other specialists.

Before any problem can be solved, it must first be accurately identified.

Every business has problems. Feel free to call it want you want: challenges, difficulties, issues, etc. Great leaders and great companies learn to work through them quickly and efficiently. Exceptional company owners encourage their team members to bring up these problems at regular meetings (more on meetings later).

Once revealed, follow the **three Ds**:

Discover what the real problem is.

Discuss all possible solutions.

Deal with it.

Discover—This is the *key* to problem solving! You must spend adequate time exploring what the real problem is. If you don't identify *the root cause*, then you'll waste time looking to treat a symptom.

Discuss—This involves first creating an atmosphere that welcomes all ideas (without judgment). Discussion opens up the potential of solutions that might be overlooked otherwise.

Deal—Once a solution is decided on, someone needs to take responsibility/ownership in the correction process. This person or team must be resourced to achieve the goal and a timeline put in place.

ACTION STEPS

1. Establish a culture of trust where everyone feels safe identifying and bringing problems to the attention of their leaders and team members.

2. Quickly deal with problems to keep them from getting worse.

3. Look beyond the symptoms for the real cause of the problem.

4. Determine the best solution(s) and implement it quickly.

7. The Process

*You cannot improve a process if you
don't know what the process is.*

A key element of *Kaizen*—a Japanese business philosophy—is continuous improvement.

THREE TYPES OF PROCESSES

1. **Your Unique Process**—(The 30,000-Foot View) How your company provides its services or products to your customers.

    i. This may require some deep thought and even some help from a consultant to discover the way you deliver your services or products to your clients/customers that *differentiates* you from your competitors.

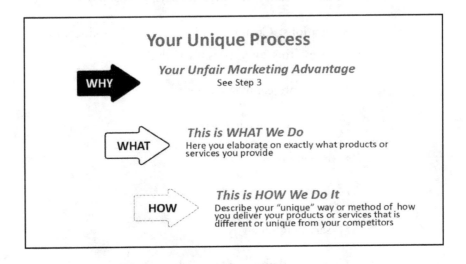

The Benefit: Your Unique Process causes you to stand out from your competitors and gain a greater advantage on why potential customers should choose you.

2. **Core Processes**—(The Mountain Top View) These are the five to ten key processes that, together, make the company run efficiently and with maximum profit.

   i. These key processes essentially divide the whole (your company) into the different parts that, when efficiently working together, create a highly productive and profitable business.

   ii. They may include the following:

      1. Lead Generation: Marketing and Advertising

      2. Sales: Converting leads to paying clients/customers

      3. HR: Hiring, Firing, Promoting, Rewarding

      4. Finance: Collecting revenue, paying bills, payroll

      5. Operations: Creation and Delivery of products or services. This could possibly include:

         • team/project management

         • inventory management

         • distribution

         • installation

         • servicing/repair

      6. Company Culture: Designed to improve retention, boost productivity, and increase individual growth

7. Leadership Development: Training designed to edify all team members and fast-track upward movement of motivated individuals

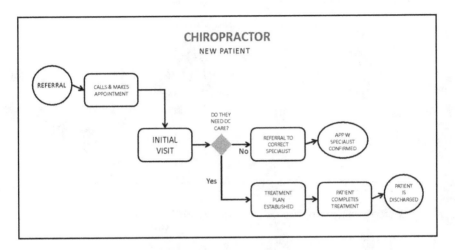

The Benefit: Knowing your "Core Processes" allows you to focus on the key areas that increase profits and boost efficiency. Without this in place your resources may be poorly focused and as a result your margins shrink without you being able to locate the source.

3. **Individual Processes**—(A view from the trenches) These document the step-by-step details of what a team member does in their specific role.

   i. These are more granular by nature

   ii. They may be tied into their scorecard

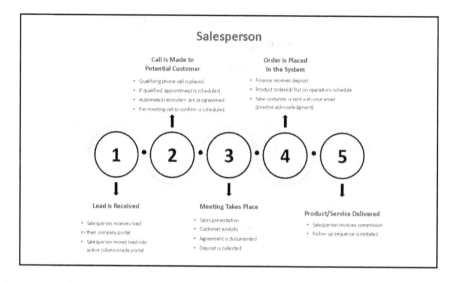

Every person that works as part of your team fits in *one or more* places on your organizational chart.

Each job position should have a documented (written or video), step-by-step description of what they do and how they do it. (It's critically important that they know WHY it is important to the whole of the company/business.)

ACTION STEPS

1. If your team member is experienced and does their job well, ask them to write a description of what they do and how they do it in a step-by-step order.

2. These steps don't need to be too granular (micro details) but rather need to capture the necessary things they do and the proper sequence (if applicable).

3. If this job is new, then you'll need to do your best to outline the steps you know are needed. Once someone is in this role, they can help you refine the process.

4. Once the process is clearly understood, it needs to be written down and kept as a living document (one that will be revisited often and tweaked if necessary).

5. If you really want to take it to the next level, video record the process. This will allow you to build a library of training tools to train new team members. This maximizes efficient and consistent training. The great news is that video documenting is relatively inexpensive. Using a smart phone and screen capturing software will typically do the job.

The Benefit: When a team member leaves or is moved to another role, this documented process increases the speed of training a new team member, shortens their learning curve, and maintains consistency in that job role.

On March 13, 2019, Gallup published an article, "This Fixable Problem Costs U.S. Businesses $1 Trillion." In it, they cite that the 2017 Bureau of Labor Statistics reported a 26.3 percent employee turnover rate in the United States at an average replacement cost of one half to two times the employee's annual salary.

8. Identifying Opportunities and Threats

Once you have clearly established, charted, and documented your process, it's time to identify every area of opportunity to create an "extraordinary customer experience."

It is also critical that all areas of potential threats are identified and addressed from two perspectives:

1. Proactive measures to avoid the threat

2. Mitigating actions when the threat becomes a reality

Let's take a look at the example above of the process we identified for the Salesperson. First, let's identify the OPPORTUNITIES.

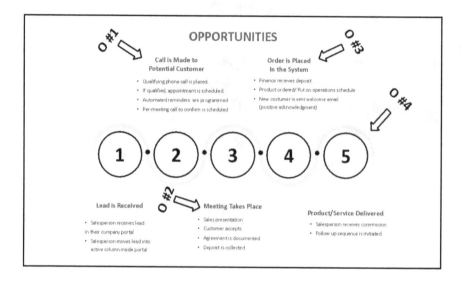

OPPORTUNITIES (O)

O#1

- Respond *immediately* (or as quickly as humanly possible) to the lead.

- Put the *needs* of this potential client/customer above yours and make sure it is clearly communicated to them.

- Accommodate their schedule as much as you can.

- Make a small promise to them and fulfill it ASAP.

O#2

- Call ahead to reconfirm the appointment (Sound excited).

- Show up early (5–10 minutes).

- Thank them for their time.

- Be well dressed/groomed (FIRST IMPRESSIONS).

- Smile often.

- Give them a small gift (reciprocity).

- Ask questions and listen carefully (Identify their needs and pain points).

- Repeat their needs and pain points back to them using their words and phrases.

- Have above average manners.

O#3

- Small gifts (coffee, donuts, bottles of water) to the accounting/operations teams can go a long way in keeping your customers a priority.

- Once the email is sent, text the customer/client to alert them of the email. This email outlines what has been done and what to expect next and time of process.

O#4

- Small thank you gift along with a handwritten card is either sent or preferably delivered by you personally if time permits.

- Follow up to ensure their satisfaction and answer any questions or concerns.

- Reassure them of the great investment/decision they made and how delighted you are to have served them.

This list is certainly not exhaustive; however, it's designed to stimulate your creative mind as to how you can create "WOW" into every process where it's possible.

HOW CAN YOU TURN WHAT IS ORDINARY INTO THE EXTRAORDINARY?

Free Video Training: "The Greatest Opportunity" to WOW, *https://vimeo.com/463121937.*

Let's now consider the same process and identify all potential threats.

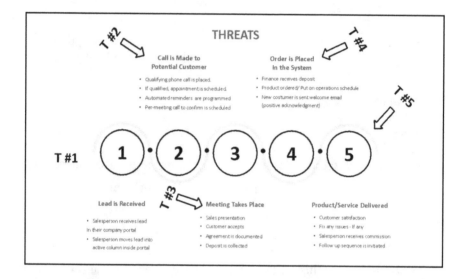

THREATS (T)

T#1

- Lead is not posted or assigned immediately.

- Salesperson doesn't have a system to be alerted and immediately respond to lead.

- Lead is seen by salesperson but not acted on.

T#2

- Client doesn't answer, a message is left, and no follow up measures are implemented

- Client doesn't answer and *no* message is left, plus no follow up is implemented.

- Poor scripting and or poor tonality on first call (FIRST IMPRESSIONS).

T#3

- arrive late

- poor body posture

- sloppy appearance

- unprepared

- talk too much/poor listening

- curt or rude attitude

- weak closing skills

- deposit not collected

- wrong price given

T#4

- Deposit is lost or delayed in turning in (Needed to get the operations process started).

- Finance and/or operations drop the ball.

- Wrong product is ordered.

- Product is out of stock (on backorder) and nobody contacts the customer.

- Operations (installation/delivery) is backed up and will create an unexpected delay. This is not communicated to the customer.

T#5

- unprofessional delivery/installation

- wrong product

- defective product

- damage to customers premises during installation

- final payment is different than quoted

- customers final balance doesn't clear (insufficient funds)

While these examples of Opportunities and Threats are not exhaustive, they should put you on the right track of building systems that take these into account.

Note: Take time to list out all the areas in your process threats and think of *proactive measures* you can create to prevent breakdown in the flow. Also, what measures will you take once the breakdown occurs?

The Benefits to mastering these areas are often greatly underestimated: Higher retention of team members, lower team turnover, increase in the lifetime value of a customer, boosted referrals (ZERO-costs customers), improved culture, less stress, and greater margins.

ACTION STEPS

1. With your leadership team, use the examples above to draw out your process.

2. If you want to get the maximum results, consider creating process charts for individual team members.

3. Work through and identify all potential places of threats or opportunities for creating WOW experiences.

4. Brainstorm how to prevent problems in areas of potential threats as well as strategies on how to recover once they occur.

5. Repeat the process in step 4 with potential areas to create extraordinary experiences with your team and customers.

6. Document and review often.

9. Building and Maintaining Growth

Once your Business Operating System is in place, it's time to put in powerful guardrails to ensure continued growth and the ability to maintain the quality of service and products.

Three factors to keep in mind to successfully complete your *1-Year Plan*:

- Consistency

- Feedback

- Unity

The way this is accomplished best is through two types of VITAL MEETINGS. Most team members dislike (even hate) meetings. The problem here lies in several areas:

- Most meetings are poorly run and very unproductive.

- No one has clearly communicated that the health of the company is directly related to these vital meetings.

- The leadership has no (or poor) regard for such meetings.

THE TWO TYPES OF VITAL MEETINGS

- Quarterly

- Weekly

QUARTERLY MEETINGS

The Why:

- The 90-Day action plan that serves to help fulfill the *1-Year Plan*

The What:

- Every 90 days (No Excuses)

- One to two days, preferably off site

- Includes All Key Team Members (owners and team leaders from each department)

The How:

- Have a good note taker. (Could be a professional hired for just these meetings)

- Have a clear agenda and rules to govern the meeting.

- Each meeting should be designed to *Identify, Discuss, Measure, and Establish* the three to seven *Key Items* that will move the company toward successfully completing the *1-Year Plan*.

- All Key Items not completed (set in the previous quarter) must be discussed. Why was it not completed, who was responsible, and what needs to be done now? This is rolled forward as a Key Item for this new quarter.

- Each team leader will have their own Key Items. These are designed to support the three to seven Key Items chosen for the company.

- Raise *Key Issues* (problems) that need to be addressed.

  - Discern the root cause (not the symptoms).

  - Brainstorm all possible solutions until a consensus is reached.

  - Determine the how, who, and when for the solution.

- For each of the Key Items on the list for the new quarter, teams or individuals need to be assigned. Timelines, resources needed, and people required should be clear.

WEEKLY MEETINGS

The Why:

- Here the purpose is to stay on track in order to achieve the Quarterly Key Items.

- It is vital to stay focused in order to solve Key Issues and keep communication clear.

The What:

- The principle players here are the Owners and the Team Leaders.

- The frequency is once per week and should be the same day and time of the week.

- The meeting should take place within the office (in a room where there will be no interruptions).

- The length of the meeting should be one to two hours.

The How:

- Have an agenda and a person designated to implement the agenda to keep the meeting moving forward.

- Scorecard: A review of where everyone is at to help ensure accountability and momentum.

- Key Issues: Most of the meeting will be spent here. To avoid wasting time, identify the *root cause,* then have the discussion on potential solutions. There must be an atmosphere of openness to foster full participation (spirited debate can be healthy).

- A to-do list is created and specific people (or teams) are assigned the responsibility. Timelines and resources and help needed are determined.

The Benefits of scheduled and disciplined meetings are greater traction toward your 1-Year Plan. Those companies that adhere to the weekly and 90-Day system outperform those that don't 10:1 (my estimates).

ACTION STEPS

1. Schedule your first (or next) 90-Day meeting.

2. Plan it for one to two days.

3. Include your leadership team.

4. Depending on your budget, have it off-site with your leadership team.

5. Plan your agenda.

6. Have a note taker.

7. Assign someone to be a timer (stay on time).

8. Stay focused on the current subject and refuse to get sidetracked.

9. Have dinner and lunch together to build stronger community.

10. Repeat action steps 5–8 for weekly meetings. Most of your time should be spent on solving problems.

STEP 3—CREATE YOUR "UNFAIR MARKETING ADVANTAGE"

I took just under 18 minutes to create a permanent shift in the way I would forever see marketing and advertising.

It was 2009, and I had just watched my first TEDx Talk. In the event you've never heard of it, the TED stands for Technology, Entertainment, Design. These short presentations (18 minutes or less) cover a wide variety of topics from science to business to global issues.

It was then I realized why, for the prior two-and-a-half decades, my marketing efforts and dollars had had such a poor return on investment (ROI).

I had been doing it all wrong!

With all my knowledge of anatomy, physiology, orthopedics, and neurology, the secret was right there in front of me—I just couldn't see it, not until I watched this short presentation. Simon Sinek's (TEDxPuget Sound) talk, "How Great Leaders Inspire Action" (as of May 2020, it has had 49,986,572 views), ignited a new way of understanding how people are motivated. Sinek claimed the answer was rooted in biology.

For the first time, I knew all my marketing and advertising was appealing to the wrong part of my target audience's brain. I was competing as a *commodity* (I'll come back to this later).

In that same year, Sinek released his book, *Start with Why*. (This book is still one of my top-10 recommendations for business owners and leaders). His book expanded on this powerful concept and helped make him a popular speaker and consultant.

Sinek helped me understand that I was *leading with the wrong information!*

Pay Attention: What I'm about to explain to you has massive potential for maximizing the ROI on your marketing dollars.

Let me give you my biggest takeaways:

- Not everyone is your ideal client.

- You need to cut through the sea of "white noise" that's competing for your ideal customers' attention. Use communication that bypasses their *conscious brain* and speaks to their *emotional brain.*

- Tell people WHY you do what you do before you tell them *What* you do, and *How* you do it.

- The WHAT and the HOW speak mostly to the thinking brain (conscious thought) while your WHY bypasses consciousness and is registered in the (unconscious) emotional centers.

- Simon describes the "Golden Circle" (see below). Most companies and business owners get it in the wrong order.

- All your marketing should *lead with your* WHY. Then you follow up with your WHAT and your HOW.

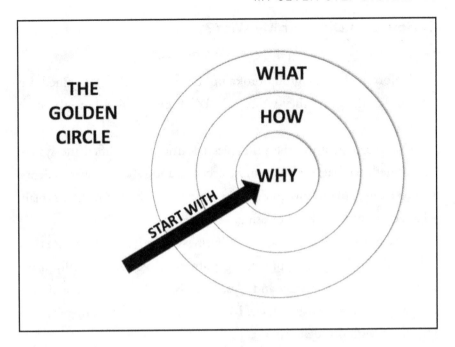

Sinek's work left entrepreneurs like me excited about the WHY concept, but failed to show how to discover your WHY, and more importantly, how to effectively apply it.

Several years later, I met a group of professionals that took Sinek's work and created a systematic approach to discovering your WHY and learning how to build your marketing message around it. They launched a training program on how to *Discover, Build, and Implement* your WHY. The goal was to target the business/corporate world on paying to be coached through this process.

Let's Explore How To

- *discover* your WHY

- *build* Your WHY

- *implement* Your WHY

1. How Do I Discover My WHY?

I was in the first group of "Certified WHY Coaches."

Unfortunately, the group broke up, but the knowledge I gained was invaluable. The book they wrote, *The WHY Engine,* is still available on Amazon.

Over years of using the principles I learned, I modified the system into something that, for me, is more accurate and is better for my clients. Before I can explain how to discover your WHY, I need to first explain what definition of WHY I'm using.

I've attended literally a 100+ business meetings, conferences, or seminars where a person presenting puts up a picture (typically using PowerPoint) of their family and says, "This is my Why." The use of *Why* here is synonymous with *purpose.* It's important to note that there's nothing wrong with this definition.

For our purposes, I'll be using a different definition.

Every computer has an operating system that it uses to process information. From the time we are young, our brain is adapting to the input from our environment. The combination of our genetics and the environment we are exposed to begins early on to form a way of processing information that our brain defaults to at a subconscious level.

Think of your WHY like the lens you see the world through. It helps steer the way you see things, and subsequently, the way you respond. It is your gift!

The mentors I studied under to get my "WHY Coaching" certification had interviewed a large number of people over several years and observed nine typical patterns they call WHYs. (for more information, go to *www.whyinstitute.com*)

The 9 WHYs

1. *Contribution*—You are hardwired to want to impact the world in a way that *makes a difference.*

2. *Think Differently*—You first see what others typically don't. You're able to see things from a perspective most aren't capable of.

3. *Make Sense*—You need to first understand the complex, and then break it down to an easy-to-understand version.

4. *Better Way*—You are always looking for a better way to do something.

5. *Right Way*—You are driven to do things the right way.

6. *Clarify*—You need clarity in order to respond appropriately.

7. *Simplify**—You operate best with simplicity.

8. *Mastery*—You are driven to learn everything you can about something that captures your interest.

9. *Trust*—You build relationships through trust. You feel extremely hurt when your trust is violated.

> * Because of their similarities, I don't use
> "Simplify" because, in my experience,
> it is indistinguishable from "Make Sense."

We all have more than one type of WHY operating in our lives, however, one or two will usually dominate.

It should be noted that the 9 WHYs have no hard science behind them. It was derived through the observation of a few men seeking to find a "better way" to help people discover their WHY.

Gerald Zaltman is the Joseph C. Wilson Professor Emeritus at Harvard Business School and the author and editor of 20 books. When his 2003 book, *How Customers Think: Essential Insights into the Mind of the Market*, was published, Zaltman's research revealed that, while people think they buy based on logic, their purchasing decisions were primarily influenced at a subconscious level.

If you're paying attention, you'll begin looking at what subconscious triggers move your customers to purchase from you and make sure your marketing targets these.

Over the past few years, I have helped hundreds of men and women uncover their WHY using a modified method of what I first learned. I discovered that by asking questions and listening to the words someone uses, certain patterns emerge that help me lock in on their most dominant WHY.

The method I initially was taught took about 20–30 minutes to discover someone's WHY. Because I'm "Results Driven," I realized the more time I spent getting to know the business owner, their business, and the team behind them, the better I was able to help them develop an "Unfair Marketing Advantage" that would easily separate them from their competition.

I deal mostly with business owners who are focused on providing products or services to the marketplace that help people. It's not hard to imagine that the WHY that drives most people that go into business is "Contribution" or "Making a Difference." A good consultant will not only help you discover your primary WHY, they'll also help you find the other WHY or WHYs that help you achieve this primary gift.

Discovering My WHY

Two of the men that wrote *The WHY Engine* and launched the "WHY Coaching Program" were Dr. Gary Sanchez and Ridgely Goldsborough. They each took me through the WHY discovery process separately and came up with different results. One said it was "Contribute," the other said it was "Make Sense."

At first, I was confused, but as I learned more about how to drill down to my actual WHY, I realized that my biggest driver is to *"Contribute to others and the world."* Here's the cool part: I contribute or make a difference by taking things that are complex and making them easy to understand (*Make Sense*).

As a doctor, postgraduate teacher, restaurateur, real estate investor, and over the past decade, as a professional speaker/business consultant, I am driven to impact people's lives for the better.

Remember my story about "Joe C" and the powerful shift my experiences with him created. It was the catalyst that began my developing the skill set of taking information I found complicated and working hard to deconstruct it into easily understood chunks. Over decades, my ability to take on more and more information and *make sense* of it grew. I was initially motivated to learn from the best sources, then quickly applied the important pieces in my life and business.

Today, I make my living doing two things: speaking and consulting. My consulting business includes components of coaching and mentoring.

I spend between two and four hours learning daily. My studies are focused in five main areas: Spiritual, Business/Financial, Relationships, Health, and Leadership.

My first priority is always on my spiritual growth. I use books, audio recordings, videos, online courses, live and virtual seminars, mentors, and one-on-one interactions as modalities of learning.

ACTION STEPS

1. Review the 9 WHYs above and take time to think about how these show up in your life.

2. Which WHY do you think is your primary way of seeing the world?

3. Is there a second WHY that helps you fulfill your primary WHY?

4. Take a few days (even a few weeks) to see if the primary and secondary WHYs you believe describe you are accurate.

5. You'll need to remain flexible and honest about your observations of your words and behaviors. It's very easy to choose a WHY we want to be true about ourselves and look only at evidence that confirms it (confirmation bias).

This is why clients hire me: I spend the time and money to learn from the best sources then turn that knowledge into actionable strategies to implement for fast results.

2. How to Build Your WHY

Once you've discovered your WHY, it's time to craft it into a message. I have seen this done two different ways.

One, you tell your story and how your journey led you to your current business and purpose. This can be quite effective when it's kept short enough not to bore your target customer, and you can clearly connect your journey to your purpose.

The second is my preferred method:

1. Discover your WHY. (You can hire a consultant/coach to help you or go to *www.whyinstitute.com* and take the automated test.)

2. Craft your WHY into a few paragraphs (at most) using words that immediately speak to the "emotional" centers (unconscious) of your ideal client.

3. Be able to speak it in one minute or less.

Earlier I said I would circle back to tell you the reason to avoid being a commodity!

I practiced as a Doctor of Chiropractic in the '80s and '90s in Sarasota, Florida. It's hard to imagine there being NO INTERNET; however, the most common advertising methods were the Yellow Pages, newspapers, magazines, radio, TV (very expensive), and billboards.

Imagine it's 1988, and you just moved to a new town. You haven't met anyone yet, and your back is hurting badly from lifting tons of boxes. The previous owners left you a copy of the Yellow Pages so you pick it up and search for a good chiropractor. For the most part, every ad looks the same, except for the size and whether it includes color.

Each ad would include features like these:

• What school the chiropractor graduated from

• What technique and therapies are used

• If insurance is accepted

• If workers' comp, auto accident, sports injuries, etc., are accepted

• Maybe a picture of the chiropractor or a patient testimonial

Your choice will be most likely based on proximity to your home or some other random reason. All they communicated is their WHAT and HOW. They (including me) never told you our WHY.

I'm sure by now, you understand that you need to stop competing as a commodity and laser-target your customer's brain to elicit an emotional reaction at an unconscious level.

Let me bring this concept home with two examples, each appealing to a different area of the brain. Your job will be to choose which one would get your attention best.

Here's the setup.

I (Dr. Ron) have been invited to pitch my consulting services to 100 large companies looking for help from someone like me. There are nine other consultants that will also pitch this group with the goal of getting their business.

We each were given one minute only.

I am deciding between two pitches. Here they are:

PITCH #1

Hi, my name is Dr. Ron Eccles. As a business consultant for the past decade, I've worked with many companies like yours. We specialize in boosting revenue, cutting waste, and increasing your profitability. Over the years, I built a proven "Seven-Step System" to help you grow and scale your company. My experience includes having built multiple six- to seven-figure businesses over the past four decades. My clients range from teams between three to several hundred. I have a small dedicated team of professionals that are ready to serve your business needs. If you're looking for a consultant that is experienced and is dedicated to growing your company, please see me afterwards. Again, my name is Dr. Ron Eccles.

PITCH #2

I wake up every day with a burning passion inside me. I am driven to help men and women achieve everything in life you were made for. You see, I know the sacrifices each of you has made to build your company to where it is today. I also fully understand the daily challenges and obstacles you face to scale your business in the presence of growing competition, an increasing age diversity of your team members, and shrinking margins.

I have had the honor of working with dozens of men and women like you, helping them get the long deserved breakthroughs they sought after. Isn't it time you close the gap in your life and business, and experience your God-given potential? If you're looking for the right consultant that's equally committed to your business and personal success, please see me afterwards. My name is Dr. Ron Eccles.

If you were one of the company owners looking to hire a business consultant, which would get your attention best?

I'm assuming most of you reading this book would choose Pitch #2 because it appeals to your emotional centers first. This is where most people make their buying decisions, then justify their decision logically.

Pitch #1 sounds pretty good, however, the other nine consultants will list out their resume. I would be one of 10 commodities to pick from. Pitch #2 clearly separates me from the other nine.

OK, now you understand how to "Discover your WHY." It's time to *Build your WHY* into a message.

ACTION STEPS

1. Set aside some uninterrupted time over a period of two days, about two hours each day.

2. Write out "your story." Don't write a novel and be careful not to place yourself as a "victim." Journal the highlights and key events.

3. Writing your story may bring up strong emotions (negative and positive). Make sure you're in a safe place when you do this and avoid doing this activity if you're feeling mentally and emotionally vulnerable.

4. If you begin to experience any painful memories that are unresolved, make sure you have someone to talk to or counsel with. Seeking professional help is a great way to assist you in dealing with unresolved emotions. You may even look for programs through your church. My church has "Freedom Groups" that have helped many people deal with unresolved pain from their past.

5. Once your story is written, take time to review it looking for key patterns that helped shape the reason you're in your current business. Sometimes it's difficult to see a direct connection and requires a deeper dive to look for underlying patterns that have influenced your current position.

6. You are now ready to craft your WHY. Write it out and don't worry if it's not smooth at first. You can mold and modify it over time.

7. Start practicing telling others your WHY; it's the fastest way to hone it into a powerful and clear message that will give you that "Unfair Marketing Advantage."

3. How to Implement Your WHY

Growing up in New Jersey in the '60s and '70s, with a family heritage of Irish, English, and Scottish, didn't expose me to much diversity in food. We were typical meat-and-potatoes people. My neighborhood was fairly diverse; however, most of my friends were of Italian descent. Their mothers were either immigrants or first-generation American, and they were all incredible cooks.

Early on in life, pizza became my favorite Italian meal. The New York/New Jersey area was rich with incredible pizzerias. I bet you can instantly name your favorite pizza restaurant.

Starting in the mid-'90s, I owned and operated several pizza restaurants for about a decade. Pizza has three main ingredients: dough, sauce, and cheese. It was my experience that there is one of these that people use first to judge how much they enjoyed the pizza.

As a business owner think of your WHY as the "main ingredient" to all your marketing and advertising. If you get this right, the ROI on your marketing and advertising efforts will skyrocket.

The question my clients always ask at this point is *where* and *how* do we implement this game changer?

The "where to implement" question is easy to answer. Everywhere!!!

- Your Company Wall (or Your Home Office)

- Your Website

- Your Brochures

- Your Business Social Media Channels

- TV, Radio, Podcasts, Webinars

- Public Speaking

- One-on-One

- All Phases of Your Team Members' Journey

- Letterhead, Business Cards, Promotional Items

Are you getting the picture?

You want to always lead with your WHY. It's the way to instantly connect with your ideal client. You should also consider the opposite truth. You will repel those who do not resonate with your WHY.

Now we need to address the *how* question.

Determining the how depends on which medium you're implementing your WHY in. You will use a short, powerful WHY message that quickly appeals to the emotion centers. If more is needed, you can tell about your journey to your current business.

Creativity is definitely needed in this part. Working with a seasoned professional in the WHY process can facilitate your results. I brainstorm with my clients on creating their different-length messages for different marketing channels. After tackling a few together, they begin to catch the pattern and usually take it from there. Once they (working with their team) have nailed version 1.0, they seek my opinion.

Note: Perfection is the enemy of progress! You will enhance your WHY over time as you master the core concepts. You'll see how most businesses are competing as commodities and wasting valuable marketing dollars.

Every once in a while, you'll see someone get it right, and you'll get excited because you now know the difference, and more importantly, your confidence in your WHY grows.

Back to pizza!

With a decade of owning and operating multiple pizza restaurants, I'm convinced that the crust (cooked dough) is the main determining factor (main ingredient) in how people experience their favorite pizza. Look, I realize that you might think that the sauce or the cheese is the main ingredient, and that's certainly your right. *The principle is to tell people your WHY before your How or What.*

Your WHY gives you that "Unfair Marketing Advantage" you've been looking for. Now it's time to learn how to increase the lifetime value of each customer and how to get new clients at ZERO cost.

ACTION STEPS

1. Make a list of all your marketing channels (website, social media, direct mail, brochures, podcasts, public presentations, etc.).

2. Look for opportunities to lead with your WHY.

3. Getting your ideal client to pay attention to your message over that of everyone else competing for their attention is the main focus.

4. Do your best to build your WHY into every possible facet of your marketing.

5. Teach all team members to communicate your company WHY clearly and effectively.

UNSTOPPABLE SUMMARY:
CREATE YOUR UNFAIR MARKETING ADVANTAGE

Discovering your WHY sets you apart from your competitors.

Turning your WHY into an effective message speaks directly to your ideal clients emotional brain, bypassing their conscious brain.

Inserting (and leading with) your WHY into all your marketing gives you that "unfair advantage."

When your team knows the WHY of the company (typically your WHY) and buys into it, everyone knows how to express the WHY to build momentum.

STEP 4—CRAFT AN EXTRAORDINARY EXPERIENCE

He had me at "free patients"!

Immediately upon graduating from chiropractic college in 1983, I joined a practice management group called Charting to learn how to grow a successful practice. I graduated with just under a 3.5 GPA but I had absolutely NO EXPERIENCE with building and running a chiropractic practice. I've heard it said, "If you think education is expensive, try ignorance."

I've always been grateful for the money I invested in my education. My favorite instructor in chiropractic school and at Charting was Dr. Roy Hillgartner. He was one of those uniquely gifted individuals that excel at both practicing and teaching.

I learned many incredible lessons from all of my mentors; however, it was Dr. Hillgartner that taught me the most powerful secret on how to get a consistent flow of new patients (customers) at ZERO COST.

In STEP 2, I laid out 9 Key Components. Seven and eight showed you how to document your processes (core and individual) and identify areas of threat and opportunity.

I want you to divide your business into two buckets. In bucket one, you have all your current clients (or however you label them). In bucket two, are all of your team members.

Here's the secret: Crafting an Extraordinary Experience is the "BEST WAY TO FILL YOUR BUSINESS WITH THE *BEST CUSTOMERS AT ZERO COST.*"

Start with Your Current Clients

1. Your job is to lay out your customer journey (process) from beginning to the end.

2. Get as detailed as possible identifying all the touchpoints (interactions that are organic to the process).

3. Think of ways (nonorganic) that you can insert as additional experiences to WOW your customer.

   Example: At my restaurants, we collected email addresses along with their birthdays and anniversaries. We would email them a coupon for a free 12" pizza for each.

4. Put yourself in your customers' place to see what would be an extraordinary experience to them.

   Example: I spent time getting to know my private (one-on-one) clients and I would send gifts that were meaningful to them. Oftentimes, I would send a birthday gift for their spouse or child.

5. Do your best to identify the person or department responsible for each interaction.

   Example: During my years in practice as a chiropractor, my team was trained to use their position to identify anything important about our patients (good and bad news) and communicate it to me. Sometimes my patients would tell my team difficult things they were going through that they didn't want to bother me with. When my team member relayed the information to me, I would respond to make sure they knew how much we cared about them.

6. Brainstorm ideas to use that opportunity to create an AMAZING EXPERIENCE. Get your team involved in coming up with as many creative ways as possible to blow your clients out of the water.

   Example: When I was in the restaurant business, I regularly looked for opportunities to turn a complaint into an experience that was aimed at creating a "loyal customer." I would apologize for the issue, and usually remove the charge and replace the meal at no charge, or in the case of food we delivered, I would credit their account for the full amount. My managers and wait staff had full authority to do the same.

7. Immediately implement these ideas. Carefully document them and include who is responsible. Add this to their "scorecard" (previously discussed).

8. I recommend gamifying this process and consider adding some healthy competition to fortify the concept.

   Example: I have recommended to many of my clients to implement a voluntary book-reading program. I suggested books that would build them up personally and professionally. Having a scoreboard with pages read each week can create healthy competition and fun. You could also have a private Facebook Group for those participating asking them to post videos and comments on how they're implementing the ideas and strategies. Have a monthly lunch (paid for by the company) where you discuss the book and everyone votes on the best takeaway posted in the Facebook Group with a small prize.

9. Discuss the results during your weekly meetings.

10. During your 90-Day meetings, discuss what is working, what needs improvement, and new ways to implement.

Your Team Members

- Use your leadership team to help you.

- Document their journey, from the hiring process to the time they leave your company. (Your goal is to hire the right people for the right job.)

- Look for every touchpoint to create extraordinary experiences for your team members (organic and nonorganic).

- Document the experience process and identify who is responsible.

- Consider creating a checklist for each team member so you can actually measure what you're doing, how often, and their response.

- Review the results in your 90-Day meeting. Discuss what's working, what needs improvement, and new ideas.

Additional Comments

- Get to know your customers and team members. By uncovering their interests and likes, you can craft more individualized experiences.

  Harvey Mackay, author of *Swim with the Sharks without Being Eaten Alive,* created the Mackay 66 for his sales team. This allowed them to build a detailed profile of their customers. Consider building a profile on your team and clients that allows you greater opportunities to build in WOW experiences.

- Think things like age, gender, years of service, and other variables when finding what excites them to know how to craft the experience.

WHY THIS STEP IS SO IMPORTANT

- Referrals are ZERO-COST-TO-ACQUIRE customers.

- Since they come from loyal customers and team members, there is automatic trust and they are typically your best customers.

- The more referrals you get, the lower your overall "cost to acquire" a customer is. This can have a powerful impact on boosting your margins (profits).

- These referred customers are "pre-framed" to like your company, and in return, will refer others to you.

- When you regularly focus on these principles, it creates an increasing momentum for more and more Zero-Cost customers.

Dr. Hillgartner taught me the secret to getting patients at no cost by getting my existing patients to refer their family members, friends, coworkers, and anyone they meet that might need my services. The key was to ask for the referral at the right opportunity.

Most patients came to me with pain they couldn't get relief from. As soon as they reported a positive result (typically one to two visits), I made sure I took the opportunity to celebrate with them, anchoring the experience deep into their subconscious mind.

I would then ask them if they would do me a big favor (law of reciprocity) by sending anyone they knew to me that might need my services. Everyone would say yes!

I would then shake their hand, warmly holding it with both of mine. I would lock eyes with them and say, "You promise?" . . . They would respond, "Yes." . . . I would slightly increase the firmness of my grip and say, "I have your word?" . . . They would once again say, "Yes" . . . Followed by me saying, "Great! It's a deal."

I had many more great experiences built into the systems in my practice and was able to grow my income and profit each year. I didn't understand the neuropsychology of what I was doing; however, it was very effective. If I had only understood what I'm teaching you here, back then, I would have crafted many more WOW experiences then I did.

Free Video Training: "The Mobius Way—Over Delivering," *https:// vimeo.com/463097386.*

UNSTOPPABLE SUMMARY: CRAFT THE EXTRAORDINARY EXPERIENCE

1. The goal is to get referrals from your current and past customers as well as from your team. Your cost to acquire these new customers is ZERO or close to it.

2. Separate your customers' journey from the team members' journey.

3. Identify all areas of potential WOW opportunities plus areas of threat (where problems could happen).

4. Brainstorm with your team to create a list of WOW opportunities.

5. Create and document the system and procedure to achieve the experience.

6. Get feedback on what works and ideas on how to improve on it.

7. Keep score of referrals generated so you can celebrate these successes and reward the referring party.

STEP 5—BUILD AN INSPIRED CULTURE

Great Company Cultures Lead to Great Growth and Profit.

"They are lazy, stupid people!" I can't tell you how many times this business owner said this in private as well as to the people on his team.

I was a consultant/trainer for this company several years ago. This business owner was successful in growing several other businesses and had launched a new company in a different market. The market was hot for what they sold, and it was just the beginning. The company came out of the gates strong and added many new team members during the first two years as they expanded.

This owner and I became close friends as the company grew; however, the patterns and behaviors of this individual quickly emerged and team members quickly began to leave. I received feedback from many of those exiting, either directly or through another team member. None of it was good!

They all loved the company's products, vision, and mission but felt the culture was toxic. They each expressed discontent with the way they were treated by the owner and didn't see any change on the horizon.

In essence, the company culture created by the owner was killing this company!

Despite my greatest efforts, this person I called a friend wouldn't listen to my feedback or suggestions. In one of my conversations with this individual, I told them that if I charged them a LARGE consulting fee, they might have listened and changed. Things only got worse.

You will either manage your culture or it will manage you! Every company has a culture, some good, others bad.

Over the past four decades, I've seen few company cultures I would want to model. Some small business owners have only recently become aware of the importance of this "game-changing" concept but don't know how to develop it.

Ask 20 business owners to define "company culture" and you'll get 20 different answers.

Let's start by defining *culture* as it relates to any company (more commonly referred to as an *organization*).

Definition of Culture: *The spirit or personality of a company expressed by how they act and think. It is the character of the company.*

- It's the way people feel about the work they do, and the values they believe in.

- It's where they see the company going.

- It's what they're doing to get it there.

Roger Connors and Tom Smith, in their 2011 book, *Change the Culture, Change the Game* (a must-read), tell us that the secret weapon to developing a strong culture is "ACCOUNTABILITY." Greater accountability leads to game-changing results.

Accountability is the heartbeat of a strong culture. When everyone in the company is committed to the vision, mission, and core values, and lives them out, profitability soars.

There are several key ingredients to pulling this off to create sustainable growth:

- Everyone must *recognize the need* for accountability.

- When being accountable is part of your behavioral DNA, it comes from the inside out!

- When your accountability becomes *solution-focused*, it becomes *sustainable*.

- Your accountability means *no excuses, fully dependable*, and *action-oriented*.

- The way we hold one another accountable defines the very nature of our working relationships: how we interact, what we expect from one another, and how we do things around here.

- Accountability builds both individual and company success.

- Managing the culture of a business requires leaders, managers, and team members to think and act in the manner necessary to achieve desired results.

One of the Core Competencies of a Leader is to manage the business culture so that it drives results.

The Payoff of an Inspired Culture

Culture Eats Strategy for Breakfast.
Peter Drucker

Every Thursday morning at 7 a.m., I jump on a Zoom call hosted by my friend Brian Yost with City Commit (*www.citycommit.com*), a Christian ministry dedicated to impacting our local communities.

One Thursday morning, Brian asked a regular attendee of our calls, Don Vichitvongsa (Vice President of Manufacturing at PGT Innovations), to interview his boss, Jeff Jackson, CEO. PGT Innovations manufactures custom doors and windows. Headquartered in Venice, Florida, PGT has 3,500 team members across five facilities and generates about $800+ million yearly (*www.PGTinnovations.com*).

During the global pandemic caused by COVID-19, many companies were adversely impacted. Illness and death were not the only result. Lost jobs, decreased profits, and bankruptcy spread as the social distancing orders remained in place.

Listening to Jeff and Don, it was abundantly clear that PGT had their focus on putting their team members first. Their intention was to protect workers from contacting or spreading the virus at work while maintaining, as much as possible, maximum production and minimizing layoffs.

PGT immediately implemented the following measures:

- Mandatory temperature screening

- Social distancing at work, wherever possible and safe

- Cleaning and sanitizing work stations every two hours

- Wearing face masks at work

- Reduced face-to-face meetings and on-site visitors

- COVID Task Force Team meets weekly

- At-risk team members to be sent home (volunteer basis) with pay

- Anyone affected by COVID to be paid for 14 days (quarantine) until they receive a negative test

- PGT maintains the policy of working with each team member without risk of losing their job

Companies like PGT understand that the principle of placing high value on their team members (driven by company culture) has huge payoffs on lowering the tremendous cost in turnover, increasing productivity, higher quality work, and increased profit margins. From recruitment to retention to performance, company culture impacts every facet of your business.

Here are seven areas how culture impacts your business:

1. *Increased Employee Retention*—When employees are excited about their job and daily responsibilities, they are less likely to resign or quit for another job. The Work Institute conservatively estimates that the cost to lose a United States worker

is $15,000. Generalizing this cost to United States voluntary turnover in 2018, United States employers have lost $617 billion to employee turnover.

2. *Recruit Better Talent*—By creating a strong culture that cares about employee opinion, it makes outsiders want to be part of your organization. When the time comes that you do need to hire, it is easier to attract quality talent instead of the same lackluster leads. Hiring the right talent is essential to maintaining a positive culture as well as achieving goals.

3. *Improves Brand Reputation*—The way your community, whether online or local, views your business has the power to boost sales. A strong culture creates a buzz about your business in the community. When this buzz is positive, it makes a business look exceptional and makes customers want to do business with you.

4. *More Productive*—A strong company culture increases productivity within your organization in many ways. When your team members are happier, they show up consistently and take fewer sick days. Happy team members want to be at work and give 100 percent effort while they are there.

5. *Better Decision-Making*—A strong company culture includes a well-defined mission and vision. Making decisions are easier when they are filtered through the company's core values. When there is a question, any employee, manager, or leader can find the answer within these items. As a result, decisions will be better aligned with company goals and increase your chances of achieving success.

6. *Generate More Revenue*—Great company cultures makes customers want to work with you. Customer retention increases

as they establish loyalty to your brand and build relationships with your team. These loyal customers will refer others to you and are willing to spend more on products or services.

7. *Bigger Bottom Line*—Combining all of these benefits increases sales and decreases expenses on several levels, which results in more profits for your business, allowing you to outgrow your competitors.

Building a Great Company

Before I share the steps to building the company culture you desire, it's critical I walk you through my "Life's Secret Success Formula" I call *I.T.A.R.* I can't emphasize enough the importance of this formula. I've been teaching it since 2014.

This formula will be the FOUNDATION for building a Great Company Culture, developing outstanding personal and business leadership.

I'll briefly introduce it here and expand on it in Section 3 of this book. *This one formula will deliver the success you seek when you master it.*

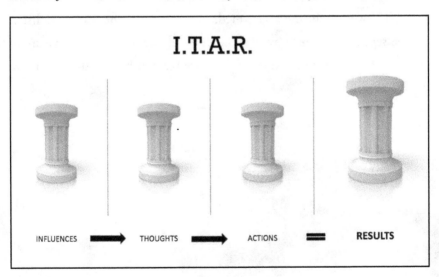

Let me start at the final component of the formula—*RESULTS*.

Everything in your life right now is a result. Your finances, relationships, health, and spiritual life are (good, bad, or in-between) simply a result.

Your *ACTIONS* produce your *RESULTS*!

Your results are less dependent on the BIG actions you take occasionally than on the small actions (habits) you practice regularly. Your actions are driven by two systems, one more powerful than the other.

Your *ACTIONS* are driven by your *THOUGHTS*!

We daily do things at both a conscious and subconscious level. According to the Coved Laboratory of Neuro Imaging at the University of Southern California, the average person has about 48.6 thoughts per minute (70,000 per day). Our dominant thoughts that are repeated with sufficient intensity (through voluntary or involuntary means) will be the ones driving our actions.

Our *THOUGHTS* are produced by our *INFLUENCES*!

What we read or don't read, who we hang out with, what and how much TV we watch, the social media we consume, the music we listen to, the seminars/webinars we watch, all mold our thought life. We are in control of most of our influences and are responsible for the results we experience.

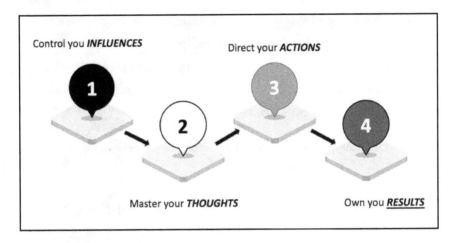

Control you **INFLUENCES**

Direct your **ACTIONS**

Master your **THOUGHTS**

Own you **RESULTS**

Building the Culture You Want

Guiding Principles of Culture Development

- The primary purpose of your business is to make disciples. The second is profit.

- Lock I.T.A.R. into your mind as I unpack the pathway to building the Company Culture you've always wanted.

- The foundation of your *Culture* will be established from your Company's Core Values.

- You must be committed to continuous improvement as time and circumstances evolve.

- Start now!

Steps for Building the Culture You Want

1. Identify what your current culture (CC) is like: It's important not to be defensive or shade the truth. Be real, raw, and transparent.

2. Define the new culture (NC) you desire. You might want to recruit the help of your team and possibly a coach to work with you on this. I suggest reading books on how leading companies create the culture they want. (Check out *Leaders Eat Last* by Simon Sinek.)

3. Document the current results you are experiencing (your current outcomes).

4. Get clear on what new outcome or new result you're committing to. (Examples: greater team collaboration, improved individual and job-related satisfaction, better buy-in to the company mission, team members caring about each other more, etc.)

5. Zero in on the current actions (CA) being taken that are generating your current results.

6. Establish the new actions (NA) needed to achieve the new result. (Examples: Set up lunches between members of different teams to develop better relationships, understanding, and cooperation.

7. What is the current thought (CT) process or mindset?

8. What new thinking (NT) is necessary to create the new actions needed? (Example: We are one company and committed to the same mission.)

9. What are the current influencers driving company thinking?

10. Establish the new influencers needed. (Example: Leadership regularly reinforces the mission of the company and affirms each person's value in fulfilling it.)

Reminder:

- What *new result* are you looking for? Perhaps it's revenue target, increase in year-to-year growth, reduction in job-related injuries, or number of units sold, etc.

- Once we define the new result we want, we then implement strategies to influence culture shift to achieve it.

Example Using I.T.A.R. to Help Us

"Begin with the end in mind" is my favorite habit to quote from Dr. Stephen R. Covey's bestseller, *The 7 Habits of Highly Effective People.*

Company: ABC Pool Service Company—Cleaning Pools, Repairing Pool Equipment

- One owner, one service manager (does all repairs), eight cleaners to service the accounts

- Current yearly revenue = $750,000; current profit margin at 36 percent = $270,000 in profit

- New result committed to 20 percent revenue growth with 20 percent ($900,000); increase in profit margin to 43 percent = $387,000 in profit

- Income source: 80 percent cleaning services, 20 percent equipment repairs

- Profit margins: cleaning services = 25 percent, equipment repairs 80 percent

Start with Results: Gather your leadership together and get clarity on your current culture and the result. Together with your team, *determine the new result you're after.* The difference between where you're at and where you want to be is called the "GAP."

Focus on Actions: What Actions are necessary?

- The company's mission, vision, and core values need to be clearly communicated to the team (owners are responsible for this).

- Release anyone who does not feel they can buy into the mission, vision, or core values of the company. (This doesn't make them a bad person. They're just not the right fit for your company.)

- Everyone needs to clearly understand and have buy-in with the new result (goal) desired.

- Positive reinforcement strategies implemented for all new results-oriented actions.

- Gamifying activities with leaderboards for all to see.

- Owner commits to setting the example to instill the new culture.

- Recruit your team into the entire process.

- Weekly pulse/90-Day meetings to reunite, reinforce, and inspire.

- Cleaners need to focus on creating opportunities to create extraordinary customer experiences to increase retention and boost referrals.

- Cleaners need to identify repairs needed and effectively communicate the needed repair to the customer in a way that creates perceived value and care.

- The owner needs to create strategies to energize and incentivize the team to bring more referrals to the company.

- The service manager/repair person should work diligently to provide fast turnaround times on repairs and create ways to create extraordinary customer experiences.

- Hire new team members that are in alignment with the vision, mission, and core values of your company.

Shift Thinking: Gain understanding of the current thinking.

- Since culture is defined as the sum of the way the team members think and behave, we must mold their collective thought process to produce the new desired actions.

- Beliefs play a critical role in both group and individual thinking. In order to make the move from the *current culture* to the *new culture* and the *current actions* to the *new actions*, there typically is a need for an upgrade in beliefs.

- The owner needs to lead the way in continually exhibiting the upgraded thinking/beliefs system. Consistently modeling this thinking and looking for opportunities to reward team members exhibiting *new thinking* behavior creates momentum for the needed shift.

Reward what behavior you want repeated.

Create Influence: The owner strategically implements new influencers to impact the NT needed.

- Team members are provided new company shirts with the company brand and a slogan to punctuate the new company culture. The new slogan is "my goal is to exceed your expectations."

- Weekly meetings include gratitude, encouragement, and input on problem solving and ways to improve.

- Owner implements a point system for gamified rewards (cash, paid time off, gift cards, etc.).

  - Number of new accounts referred by team members' efforts

  - Number of equipment repairs referred

  - Number of positive feedbacks received about a team member

  - Showing up to work early

  - Helping fellow team members

  - Living the NC values

Celebrate Results: The owner has a monthly celebration with the entire team to recognize everyone's contribution to the results achieved that month. Rewards are given out.

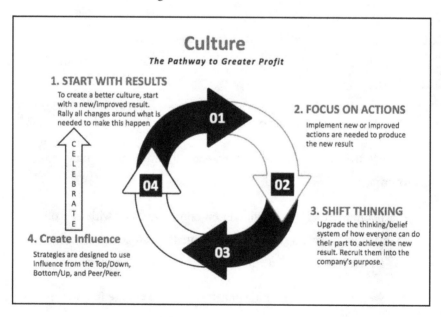

Culture

The Pathway to Greater Profit

1. START WITH RESULTS
To create a better culture, start with a new/improved result. Rally all changes around what is needed to make this happen

01

2. FOCUS ON ACTIONS
Implement new or improved actions are needed to produce the new result

CELEBRATE

04

02

03

3. SHIFT THINKING
Upgrade the thinking/belief system of how everyone can do their part to achieve the new result. Recruit them into the company's purpose.

4. Create Influence
Strategies are designed to use influence from the Top/Down, Bottom/Up, and Peer/Peer.

The Biblical-Based Culture

The Bible is the best authority we could look to for direction on building a company culture that has Kingdom results.

If we focus on the primary purpose of having a business as "making disciples," we must make sure our culture reflects Kingdom principles laid out in scripture.

Let's look at some key scriptures that will illuminate our path.

- Love one another (John 13:34, CSB; 1 Peter 4:8, CSB; Romans 12:10, CSB; 1 John 4:7–10, CSB)

- Employers to team members (Colossians 4:1, CSB; Romans 4:4, CSB; Ephesians 6:9, CSB; Proverbs 16:3, CSB)

- Team member to employer (Ephesians 6:5–8, CSB; Colossians 3:22, CSB; 1 Peter 2:18–20, CSB)

- How to do your work (Colossians 3:17, CSB; Ecclesiastes 9:10, CSB; Colossians 3:22–25, CSB; Luke 16:10, CSB; Matthew 5:16, CSB)

A culture focused first around Christ-like love creates an environment of honor toward each other, establishes a spirit of accountability, fosters trust and fairness, and sets a standard that is higher than ours.

My suggestion is to build your company core values around biblical values grounded in scripture. Here are a few ideas to stimulate your thought process.

- Love—1 Peter 4:8, "Above all, keep loving one another earnestly, since love covers a multitude of sins" (ESV).

- Respect—Titus 2:7, "Show yourself in all respects to be a model of good works, and in your teaching show integrity, dignity" (ESV).

- Honor—Hebrews 13:18, "Pray for us, for we are sure that we have a clear conscience, desiring to act honorably in all things" (ESV).

- Diligent—Proverbs 21:5, "The plans of the diligent lead surely to abundance, but everyone who is hasty comes only to poverty" (ESV).

- Proactive—Proverbs 22:3, "The prudent sees danger and hides himself, but the simple go on and suffer for it" (ESV).

- Submission—Ephesians 5:21, "Submitting to one another out of reverence for Christ" (ESV).

- Excellence—Colossians 3:23, "Whatever you do, work heartily, as for the Lord and not for men" (ESV).

- Generosity—Luke 6:38, "Give, and it will be given to you. Good measure, pressed down, shaken together, running over, will be put into your lap. For with the measure you use it will be measured back to you" (ESV).

- Service—1 Peter 4:10, "As each has received a gift, use it to serve one another, as good stewards of God's varied grace (ESV).

Free Video Training: "The Infectious Culture—The Power of One," *https://vimeo.com/461364990.*

UNSTOPPABLE INSPIRED COMPANY CULTURE SUMMARY

- Company culture drives profit.

- Love, honor, and respect are the key ingredients.

- Accountability impacts both personal and corporate profit.

- Achievement of a greater culture is centered around a new/bigger result.

- Culture is the result of groupthink and behavior.

- Shifting to a greater culture must follow the I.T.A.R. formula.

- Shaping company culture will always require new and better strategies along with updated results to build around. The foundation (mission, vision, and core values) remains unchanged.

- For the Christian-owned business, the *primary purpose is to make disciples and the key core value should be love.*

STEP 6—LEAD BY DESIGN

The greatest leader is not necessarily the one who does the greatest things. He is the one that gets the people to do the greatest things.
Ronald Reagan

Mary's (not the real name) goal was to build a multimillion-dollar company in three years, then take it to a billion within five. There was one huge problem: The growth of the company would be limited by her ability to grow her leadership skills.

I gave her a copy of John Maxwell's *5 Levels of Leadership* and asked her to read it before we discussed what changes were needed.

Leadership is INFLUENCE. In Dr. Maxwell's book, "Level 1" is the lowest type of leadership and "Level 5" is the highest.

I've given this book to most of my clients with the instructions to read it and rate their perception of how they lead (Level 1–5). Close to 100 percent of the time, CEOs and business owners rate themselves higher than their team members report. (Depending on the size of the team, I make it a point to meet with and privately interview as many as possible.)

Most business owners and CEOs I've met over the past four decades are *"Level 1,"* and I've met only a few I would consider *"Level 5"* leaders.

When I followed up with her a week later, Mary told me she had read the book and thoroughly enjoyed it. I could see that she couldn't wait to give me her number.

When asked, she proudly told me she was a "Level 5 Leader."

Mary had the kind of personality that appreciates directness. I told her that in my opinion, she was a *Level 1*!

I had taken the time to gain the trust of her leadership team where they could be honest and open with me. They revealed the reason the company was not meeting its goals.

I explained to Mary that her team was very intimidated by her and followed her only because she was the owner and they feared losing their jobs. Mary wasn't thrilled about my assessment of her leadership ability, and I could see it on her face. She looked like I just slapped her ego really hard.

There was a wide gap between where Mary's leadership ability was and where it needed to be if she wanted to build a billion-dollar-a-year business.

So what exactly is leadership?

> **Leadership** is a process of social influence,
> which maximizes the efforts of others,
> toward the achievement of a goal.

I spend a lot of time studying subjects like *leadership,* in order to help my clients learn from the best sources without having to invest the time or resources I do. I learn, summarize, and create rapid-implementation strategies for them.

John C. Maxwell is considered a top expert in the area of leadership. Maxwell explains his five levels as follows (my spin):

Level 1—Position: People follow you based on nothing more than your POSITION (owner, supervisor, manager, etc.). Team members are the least productive under this leader.

Level 2—Permission: People follow you because they like and trust you. Because they like this person, they are more productive than in Level-1 leadership. This leader doesn't possess the skills necessary to bring out the best in the team; as a result, they fail to maximize results.

Level 3—Production: Team members follow because they like this leader. This leader is skilled at maximizing production from their team.

Level 4—People Development: This leader has mastered the skill of building leaders within the organization. They spend 80 percent of the time coaching colleagues and 20 percent doing productive work. This allows them to elevate themselves to the higher and better use of their unique abilities. They typically have industry-wide impact and recognition.

Level 5—Pinnacle: Leadership based on respect. These are the leaders who are still mentioned long after they have left the organization. They are the ones who left a legacy. These are also the leaders who have spent their time actually creating leaders that create more leaders.

Leaders Eat First!

Context is everything! Simon Sinek released *Leaders Eat Last* in 2014. In an interview with a Marine Corps General, Sinek asked him, "What makes the Marines so amazing?" The General responded, "Leaders eat last."

What he meant is that if you go to any Marine Corps Chow Hall anywhere in the world, you will see the Marines lined up in rank order. The most senior person at the back of the line and the most junior person eats first. No one tells them they have to do it, and it is not in any rule book. It is because of the way they view the responsibility of leadership. Most business owners think leadership is about rank and power; Marines think of leadership as the responsibility for other human beings, that leadership and rank may not go together. So it manifests in this remarkable way.

This is what I find absolutely amazing: While Marines don't always like each other, they do *trust each other.*

Leaders in business get better results when their team members both *like*, *trust*, and *respect them.*

Every chance I get, I need to express my enormous
respect and gratitude for every man and woman that has
served or is currently serving in the United States Military
(you can substitute your Country here).
This extends to all first responders as well.
THANK YOU!!!

Here is where I want to shift context!

I believe leaders should eat first. Yep . . . that's right.

How can you pour from an empty cup?

In the early years of my coaching business, my wife referred a friend of hers to me for help (for privacy, we'll call her Emma). She was married and a mother of six children (all younger and living at home). Emma's challenge was building a team in the network marketing space.

During our first call, I wanted to build rapport and establish trust, so I asked many questions and took lots of notes. We connected quickly since I myself had five children and was a serial entrepreneur. My years of training and practice as a doctor caused me to push past her symptoms and get to the root cause. Emma told me that she believed it would be difficult to grow her business due to "not enough time." (Sound familiar?)

As I continued to ask the hard questions, she revealed her true problem. I mentioned that *"in order to have more, she needed to become more,"* so I suggested a daily self-development regime. Her pushback was immediate!

Emma said that any time spent on herself would take away from her family. I uncovered her deeper need for approval from her husband and children, driven by the constant put downs she had received from her parents and siblings throughout her life (continuing into adulthood).

My approach had to help her see herself differently and challenge her false beliefs in her time priorities. I asked her to write down a list of questions to ask some close friends. This was feedback she desperately needed. I advised her to ask for candid answers from friends she trusted. The feedback was amazing. Her friends saw her as a beautiful, kind, intelligent, and dedicated mom, wife, leader, and friend.

The bigger challenge was to get her to change her perspective on time priorities. If she continued down the path she was going, she would soon run out of gas. She needed to take time each day to fill her tank. Time in prayer, reading, building her team, exercise, and rest were tools to reenergize her. She would finally be able to *"pour herself into others from a full cup."*

Emma didn't need more time; she needed to reprioritize her use of time and change her self-image from unworthy and needy to a woman blessed and able to do amazing things all by the grace of God. Emma shifted her perspective and quickly implemented the changes she needed to succeed in her family and business life.

Emma needed to eat first!

In order to have more, you must become more!

Becoming a great leader doesn't happen overnight, it starts with *intent,* develops in *time,* and is a *continuous process.* Like a muscle, it requires regular exercise and good nutrition in order to grow.

The Marines (and all branches of the armed forces) need great leaders to ensure success. Great leaders understand that it is better to develop skilled teams that follow from an internal drive rather than from a posture of rank or position. The concept of "Leaders Eat Last" is a great example of servant leadership.

Look . . . nobody is ever at their peak 100 percent of the time. The good news is rooted in the principle of continuous progress. By working on ourselves daily to advance our leadership (and other) skills, we develop momentum as well as effectiveness in our leadership of others.

Here are four habits all great leaders follow:

1. Great leaders are also great followers. They have one or more mentors, teachers, or coaches they follow.

2. They are avid students of leadership and other great leaders.

3. They are committed to living disciplined lives.

4. Great leaders assume full responsibility; the buck stops with them.

The Unstoppable Christian Business is built on servant leadership.

Jesus is the example for us to emulate. He modeled great leadership by being totally submitted to following the leading of His Father.

Jesus was fully God and fully man. He showed us what it means to be a great follower and leader.

JESUS AS LEADER:

John 13 provides us with powerful lessons from Jesus on this subject:

The Setting: Gathered with His disciples for supper, before the Passover Festival.

Act: Jesus washes the feet of His disciples.

Context: Washing of feet was reserved for the lowliest of servants.

The Point: Jesus displayed a different view of leadership (counter-cultural). He wanted them to follow Matthew 20:26–28:

> *It must not be like that among you. On the contrary, whoever wants to become great among you must be your servant, and whoever wants to be first among you must be your slave; just as the Son of Man did not come to be served, but to serve, and to give his life as a ransom for many.*

What we can learn from Jesus in John 13:

- He was motivated by love and grace to serve.

- He served from a position of security not weakness. He knew who He was and His purpose.

- He initiated the act without waiting for cues from His surroundings or others.

- He encouraged us not to allow pride to prevent us from being served by others.

- When those in higher rank, position, or authority model servant leadership to those in lower ranks, position, or authority, it becomes the standard acceptable behavior.

- We are blessed when we obey Jesus in His call to serve others.

JESUS AS A FOLLOWER:

John 6:38, "For I have come down from heaven, not to do My own will, but the will of Him who sent Me" (ESV).

Mark 14:36, "And He was saying, 'Abba! Father! All things are possible for You; remove this cup from Me; yet not what I will, but what You will'" (AMP).

Matthew 4:3–4, "And the tempter came and said to Him, 'If You are the Son of God, command that these stones become bread.' But He answered and said, 'It is written, 'Man shall not live on bread alone, but on every word that proceeds out of the mouth of God'" (AMP)

Jesus surrendered to the will of the Father. God led, Jesus followed. The Disciples followed Jesus, Believers followed the Disciples.

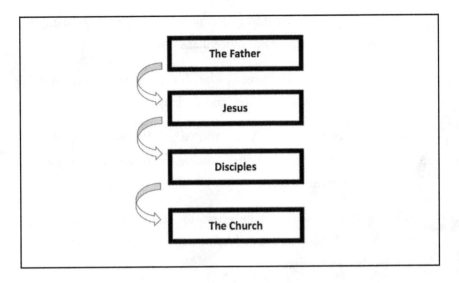

There's something about Mary. (Sorry, I couldn't help myself.) Whether you're looking to grow your business to the billion-dollar level or to six or seven figures, you must become a great servant leader. Mary needed to develop her leadership skills.

I laid out a plan for Mary to follow what I suggest for all business owners:

1.   Get Clear—Leadership is influence. You need to get clear about where you're leading your team to.

2.   Commit to Servant Leadership—Everyday your mind needs to be focused on being accountable to your team. Your job is to inspire, empower, and equip them to excel in their position.

3.   Study Leadership—What you focus on expands. Read books, listen to audios/podcasts, watch videos/YouTube, attend leadership conferences, and hire coaches. You should commit to one hour of studying leadership every other week.

4. Exceed the Losada Ratio (3:1 positive to negative)—Find ways to give positive praise/feedback often.

5. Refocus—Keep Refocusing the Team on the company's vision, mission, core values, and 90-Day goals.

6. Model and Reward What You Want Repeated—Be the example, and find ways to reinforce the behaviors that you want everyone doing.

7. Duplicate Leaders—You grow the most from teaching others. Developing other leaders increases productivity and accelerates profitability.

8. Welcome Feedback—When you genuinely seek constructive feedback on your leadership style and effectiveness, you not only create the opportunity for improvement, you also build trust.

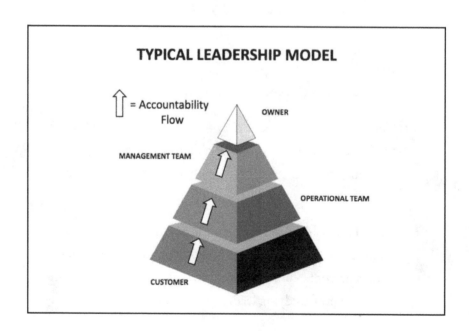

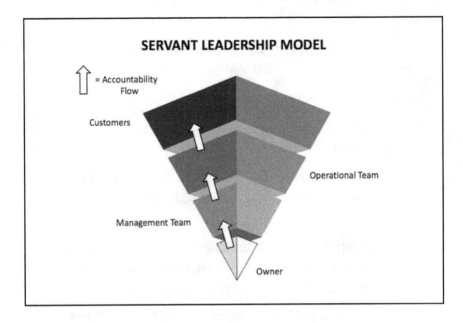

SERVANT LEADERSHIP MODEL

= Accountability Flow

Customers

Operational Team

Management Team

Owner

Leadership and Culture are closely tied together. Servant Leadership is countercultural. Turning the funnel upside down helps build an INSPIRED BUSINESS where the management team feels valued, served, and loved by the owner. They become empowered to serve the operations team, who in turn serve the client. When everyone is accountable to everyone else, company cohesion occurs, culture is elevated, and everyone operates in their giftedness to achieve the company's objectives.

Free Video Training: "Decentralized Leadership," *https://vimeo.com/461371389.*

UNSTOPPABLE LEADERSHIP
SUMMARY

- Leadership is INFLUENCE.

- Leadership isn't a genetic trait; it's a skill that needs to be developed.

- Leadership is directional—leaders cause others to follow in a specific direction toward a specific destination.

- Servant Leadership is the model—Jesus modeled leadership through service to others. When those at the top serve those below, then those below are empowered to serve each other and the client/customer.

- Leadership is a skill that can and should be developed continuously.

- Great Leaders build other great leaders.

- Before you can have more, you must become more.

ACTION STEPS

1. With your leadership team, review your company's Core Values to see if they support the leadership model of serving others. Add or modify, if necessary.

2. Have a meeting to communicate to all team members your new model and how it benefits everyone (be enthusiastic).

3. Answer any questions the team might have.

4. To get "buy-in" from your team, think about launching a challenge. Create rules and rewards for team members exhibiting the servant leadership behavior you're after. Establish a

method of documenting and keeping score. Post results where everyone can see them as they're updated. Pick a time (perhaps once per month) to give out rewards for the winner(s).

5. Reward what you want repeated! Look to catch others in the act of "servant leadership" and make a big deal out of it so other team members see and hear. This encourages more of the same behavior.

6. Make this part of your culture and you'll watch profits grow, while increasing productivity and achieving greater team cohesion.

STEP 7—GROWTH THROUGH ACCOUNTABILITY

Pornography, drugs, and money problems had driven his marriage to the brink of collapse. He reached the point where he finally realized that he couldn't do it on his own and he needed help. There were tears in his eyes and desperation in his voice as we spoke over lunch. DC was broken and decided to ask me to help him figure out how to save his marriage and family.

As a business coach/consultant, I adamantly contend that if you "build a better you, you'll build a better business." DC was no exception, only this time it meant being a better husband, father, friend, businessman, and disciple.

In our first meeting, I asked some hard questions, from a place of love and concern. I told DC that I wouldn't preach at him but I would draw all truth from scripture and relate most key issues to my personal walk with Jesus. He was in agreement.

I knew that DC's marriage problems were just the tip of the iceberg. The problems went much deeper. It started with the man.

I made no promises that I could fix his marriage; however, I did promise him that if he was willing to do the work, he would get the changes he was really after . . . real power, peace, and prosperity (I'm referring to spiritual prosperity). He was *all in*.

ROARing Accountability

Question: What's easier for you, to make a list of all your strengths or all your weaknesses?

Most people can more quickly identify what they are not good at rather than what they excel at. The challenge for many is that they lack sufficient motivation to change . . . and it gets worse.

As part of their paid membership, every Saturday morning at 7 a.m. (EST), I host a virtual meeting with a group of men who are part of our "ROAR" community. The purpose of the meeting is first to hold them accountable to the call of God on their lives, their marriages/relationships, their children, their church, and their businesses.

Once we pray to begin our time together, I ask for a brief one-minute check-in. I listen intently and watch their faces for cues. As we've grown closer to each other, greater trust has developed and more is shared. If I notice that someone has something going on but is reluctant to share, I reach out for a one-on-one call. I am accountable to them, and we hold ourselves accountable to each other.

A number of years ago, when God was leading my wife and I to lead a community of financially successful Christian Business Owners into a life of purpose, God gave me the name ROAR for our group because when lions hear an enemy invading their territory, they ROAR really loud as a warning to get out. In the same way, we encourage these business owners and their spouses (if married) to take back the territory God has given to them. We accept full authority over the territory God has given us and we will no longer yield to our sin or the devices of the enemy.

My wife, Johanna, and I are honored to lead the Lions and Lionesses (men and women) of ROAR to use the platform of the business God has given them to *first make disciples, then profit*.

Accountability is a major component of ROAR as well as all of my coaching programs. The context of accountability here is based on having people, friends, groups, organizations, or professionals in your life or business to help hold you accountable to a specific result.

Over the years of coaching and consulting, I've observed one simple truth, most people have gaps between where they are and where they want to be. Closing that gap for many requires help from a skilled professional or someone qualified to help (external accountability).

> *Give a person a fish, you feed him for a day.*
> *Teach that person to fish, you feed him for a lifetime.*
> *Chinese Proverb*

I love this proverb because it promotes a principle that can transform someone's business and life. However, there is a problem, before someone can develop the skills to "close the gap" they seek, they must be committed to the task.

Once we have committed to getting change in any area of life, we have several options:

1. We can go it alone without seeking any outside advice or direction.

2. We can seek advice which points us in the right direction. From there, we go alone.

3. We get a mentor/coach/guide to point us in the right direction, get us started, walk alongside us, and help us navigate around the obstacles until we become self-sufficient.

Option 3 is the wisest choice. Here are some typical scenarios:

- Pastors to shepherd us

- Teachers to educate us

- Trainers to help us get fit

- Diet experts to help us eat right

- Doctors to keep us healthy

- Athletic coaches to improve our performance

- Psychologists to help with mental health

- Business coaches/consultants to help us scale and grow

- Life coaches to help us balance things

- Counselors to help us improve/maintain our marriages

- Specialists to help us get free from addictions

My friend DC achieved amazing results because of his willingness to listen, receive advice, and take massive action. Today his marriage is solid, his walk with God is a priority, he is drug and porn free, and his businesses have never been better.

After years of helping men and women from all walks of life grow themselves and their businesses, I firmly believe that we need others to help us when we're sinking, stuck, confused, or not growing fast enough.

I know many of you reading this book are committed to getting the guidance you need to break through to that next level.

I believe you were born to succeed; you were designed for a deeper spiritual walk; crafted for deep, loving relationships; made to have a leaner, healthier body; and I believe you can experience financial freedom.

I believe too many of you are living below your God-given capabilities.

I wake up every day with a burning passion to see men and women like you achieve everything in life God put you on this planet for. I BELIEVE IN YOU!

I invite you to check my coaching and consulting programs at *www.drroneccles.com*.

But wait . . . there's more!

Remember way back in the beginning of this book, when I told you that there were 3 Key Components to building a successful business? We've covered the FUEL and the FRAMEWORK. Now it's time to discover the final key, "THE FIRE."

SECTION 3: THE FIRE

*The greater our self-discipline, the less
we need discipline from others.*

I'm unemployable! (Well, that's not completely true! If the hours fit my lifestyle, and the pay is big enough, I might work for you. LOL)

Inside every entrepreneur is a drive to own our own business, do something we love, control our schedule, and be financially free. Sounds so good when we start out; however, very few achieve anything close to it.

Most business owners reading this are still *trading time for dollars.*

- Your business is highly dependent on you.

- You regularly operate from one crisis to another.

- You're financially more stressed than you'd like.

Sound about right?

8

THE "YOU" FACTOR

In 2016–2017, I was spending a lot of time in Canada with Colin Sprake and his team at Make Your Mark. The goal was to learn everything necessary to bring "MYM" into the United States. While things eventually didn't work out, I was blessed to meet and befriend many wonderful Canadian entrepreneurs. I learned much from Sprake during my time with him.

I'll never forget how he would ask the room filled with business owners from all different industries this question: "What is the number one obstacle or limiting factor in your business?"

He would pause for effect as people would do their best to guess (unsuccessfully). Then he would get everyone to raise one arm high above their head and point to the ceiling, and then instruct them to re-point their finger down toward themselves. He would then say that "YOU" are the biggest impediment to the growth and success of your business!

After years of coaching/consulting business owners, all from different backgrounds, in diverse businesses, and in different geographic locations (often other countries), I know that the problems they experience are usually highly dependent on their individual disciplines (or lack of).

I have many friends that run high-level coaching programs (in various industries) ranging in cost from $14,000-$100,000. Their greatest frustrations have nothing to do with the effectiveness of their coaching and systems; it's always the student.

Bob and Ed Diamond (Diamond Law Center) are good friends of mine who run a business teaching folks to use unique strategies on making money in the "Real Estate Investing" niche. I credit Bob and Ed for not only launching my coaching/consulting business, but also providing me with a platform to begin my "professional speaking" career.

I'll never forget when Bob first shared with me that one of his biggest challenges in his teaching business was being asked questions he couldn't answer. Bob said, "They can ask me anything about real estate investing, and I can most likely answer it. The majority of questions I get are more about finding time to work on the business or staying focused and motivated. This is not my area of expertise."

That's when it hit me. This was my specialty. I was really gifted in motivating, inspiring, and equipping others to achieve more through developing the necessary disciplines. In the earlier years of my coaching business, I focused primarily on the self-disciplines that set up entrepreneurs (or anyone) for success. Over time, I developed my "Seven Steps System to a Seven Figure Business" platform. My coaching philosophy is still "Build a better You, Build a Better Business!"

Recently, my wife and I had a visitor to our home for lunch. She was visiting from the Philadelphia area and learned about me from my oldest son. She was an entrepreneur and was fascinated by my passion for helping business owners achieve their God-given potential.

It was about 30 minutes into our visit when, out of nowhere, she turned to me and said, "You're so intense. Did anyone tell you how intense you are?"

I didn't know how to respond because I wasn't sure if that was a good or bad thing. I thought for a moment, then asked her what she meant.

She told me it was a total compliment. She explained, she had rarely met someone with such focus and commitment. She found it to be inspiring and a bit intimidating at the same time.

That statement stayed with me for several days. I began to wonder how others perceived me. I began to consider if I should work harder on how I was coming across to others. And then, I had a revelation.

I was not called to be anyone else but who God made me to be. God impressed on me not to lower the bar He had developed in me over the years. He wants to use me to help others to raise the standards in their lives.

My wife has always reminded me that my well-developed discipline is a blessing but not everyone is committed to personal and business growth as I am.

God continues to work in me to have greater understanding and acceptance for people where they're at. My calling is to use my gifts to work with business owners who are ready to get outside their comfort zone to experience massive growth and achieve everything they are designed for.

Everyone I've worked with has gaps in their personal disciplines that affect their level of success in life and business. There are seven key disciplines of personal development that are required to live an optimized life.

9

THE SEVEN DISCIPLINES OF PERSONAL DEVELOPMENT

1. Spiritual

2. Growth Mindset

3. Time Priority

4. Health and Fitness

5. Generosity

6. Mastery

7. Mentorship

1. SPIRITUAL DISCIPLINE

I heard my friend Chris Widener once say, "You're going to spend a lot longer dead than alive, so you might want to consider if the decisions you make and the things you do here have any impact on where you spend eternity."

It's time to go "All In."

Pastor Mark Batterson's book, *All In*, inspired me to challenge other believers in Christ to live our lives 100 percent on purpose for God's Kingdom. We're all part of one team: His Church and we each have a specific assignment to fulfill.

What is our primary assignment . . . *to make disciples!*

In order to achieve the commission of Matthew 28:19–20 *(Go therefore and make disciples of all nations, baptizing them in[a] the name of the Father and of the Son and of the Holy Spirit, teaching them to observe all that I have commanded you. And behold, I am with you always, to the end of the age.),* we need regular spiritual practices to grow and mature.

9 Practices to Gain Spiritual Discipline

1. Prayer—Ephesians 6:18, "And pray in the Spirit on all occasions with all kinds of prayers and requests. With this in mind, be alert and always keep on praying for all the Lord's people" (NIV).

2. Study—2 Timothy 3:16–17, "All Scripture is God-breathed and is useful for teaching, rebuking, correcting and training in righteousness, so that the servant of God may be thoroughly equipped for every good work" (NIV).

3. Worship—Hebrews 12:28–29, "Therefore, since we are receiving a kingdom that cannot be shaken, let us be thankful, and so worship God acceptably with reverence and awe, for our 'God is a consuming fire'" (NIV).

4. Confessing Our Sins—James 5:16, "Therefore, confess your sins to one another and pray for one another, that you may be healed. The prayer of a righteous person has great power as it is working" (ESV).

5. Fasting—Acts 14:23, "And when they had appointed elders for them in every church, with prayer and fasting they committed them to the Lord in whom they had believed" (ESV).

6. Fellowship—Acts 2:42, "And they devoted themselves to the apostles' teaching and the fellowship, to the breaking of bread and the prayers" (ESV).

7. Rest—Matthew 11:28–30, "Come to me, all who labor and are heavy laden, and I will give you rest. Take my yoke upon you, and learn from me, for I am gentle and lowly in heart, and you will find rest for your souls. For my yoke is easy, and my burden is light" (ESV).

8. Celebration—Ecclesiastes 5:18–19, "This is what I have observed to be good: that it is appropriate for a person to eat, to drink and to find satisfaction in their toilsome labor under the sun during the few days of life God has given them—for this is their lot. 19 Moreover, when God gives someone wealth and possessions, and the ability to enjoy them, to accept their lot and be happy in their toil—this is a gift of God" (NIV).

9. Sexual Purity—1 Corinthians 6:18, "Flee from sexual immorality. All other sins a person commits are outside the body, but whoever sins sexually, sins against their own body" (NIV).

2. GROWTH MINDSET DISCIPLINE

She said, "I feel comfort in accepting my limitations."

Mark and Julia Mateer are part of the Pastoral team at Bayside Community Church in Bradenton, Florida, where Johanna and I attend. Pastor Julia heads up all the small groups (about 400) and my wife, Johanna, is part of her leadership team for women's groups.

Mark and Julia were leading us through the book, *The Ruthless Elimination of Hurry*, by John Mark Comer. During one of our Zoom calls, Pastor Julia discussed a teaching from Comer's book on accepting our limitations. She felt relieved that she was able to take pressure off of herself by not focusing on her weaknesses and spend her energies in the areas of gifting.

This is AWESOME advice when seen in its intended context by the author.

As I was listening to others in the group share what it meant to them, I had a totally different take on the idea on the subject of personal limitations. When it was my turn, I shared a different perspective that was very familiar to me.

I agreed that we should all operate mostly in the areas of our gifting (natural likes and abilities); however, the problem I see most often is that the majority of people are functioning far below their God-given capabilities. Mostly because of *self-imposed limitations*.

Your mindset can make or break you. Too often, we are completely unaware of the beliefs that are holding us back from operating in the full gifting God has for us.

Remember I.T.A.R.? Our thoughts direct our actions, and with time and repetition, produce our results. Let's take a look at mindset from two angles, the *spiritual* and the *physical*.

The Spiritual

The Bible has a lot to say about mindset. God's Word leaves no room for mental laziness. Here are a few examples:

- Romans 12:2, "Do not be conformed to this world, but be transformed by the renewal of your mind, that by testing you may discern what is the will of God, what is good and acceptable and perfect" (ESV).

- Philippians 4:8, "Finally, brothers, whatever is true, whatever is honorable, whatever is just, whatever is pure, whatever is lovely, whatever is commendable, if there is any excellence, if there is anything worthy of praise, think about these things" (ESV).

- 2 Corinthians 10:5, "We destroy arguments and every lofty opinion raised against the knowledge of God, and take every thought captive to obey Christ" (ESV).

- Isaiah 26:3, "You keep him in perfect peace whose mind is stayed on you, because he trusts in you" (ESV).

- Proverbs 3:13, "Blessed is the one who finds wisdom, and the one who gets understanding" (ESV).

- Proverbs 3:5, "Trust in the Lord with all your heart, and do not lean on your own understanding" (ESV).

- Colossians 3:2, "Set your minds on things that are above, not on things that are on earth" (ESV).

- 1 Peter 1:13, "Therefore, preparing your minds for action, and being sober-minded, set your hope fully on the grace that will be brought to you at the revelation of Jesus Christ" (ESV).

Our God has a whole lot to say about how we use our minds. He calls us to be mentally alert, sober-minded, and in alignment with the Holy Spirit's direction. We are expected never to be mentally dull. God gives us a mind but allows us to choose our mindset!

The Physical

Carol Dweck, PhD, is known for her pioneering work in psychology, especially in the areas of motivation, personality, and development. Her 2006 book, *Mindset*, revolutionized the way we understand the way we think.

Dr. Dweck has studied common ways the more successful people think compared to those who experience less success. She categorizes two types of mindsets: fixed and growth.

According to Dr. Dweck, when a person has a *fixed mindset* (FM), they believe that their basic abilities, intelligence, and talents are *fixed traits*.

People with a *fixed mindset always* want to appear intelligent because they believe that they were born with a *fixed level of intelligence* that cannot be modified. These people have a fear of looking dumb to people because they do not believe that they can redeem themselves once other people look at them as being unintelligent.

In a *growth mindset* (GM), people believe their abilities and *intelligence can be developed* with effort, learning, and persistence. Their basic abilities are simply a starting point for their potential. They don't believe everyone is the same, but they hold onto the idea that everyone can become smarter if they try.

Fixed Mindset	Growth Mindset
• Avoids Challenges	• Embraces Challenges
• Obstacles – Gives up easily	• Obstacles - Persists in the face of setbacks
• Effort – Sees as fruitless or worse	• Effort – Sees as a path to mastery
• Criticism – Ignores useful negative feedback	• Criticism - Learns from it
• Success of Others – Feels threatened	• Success of Others – Learns from it and is inspired by it
• Deterministic view of the world	• Has greater sense of free will

Adapted from Mindset: The New Psychology of Success by Carol S. Dweck

Dweck contends that we all have a mix of both fixed and growth mindset tendencies, although one will typically be more dominant. We may have a growth mindset when it comes to our business but a fixed mindset in our marriage. Maybe you tell people that you can't memorize scripture, but you can remember all kinds of facts about dozens of movies you've watched over the years.

The Christian Mindset

The God we serve has a higher standard for us. He calls us into a higher way of thinking and provides us with His Holy Spirit to help us. God requires us to be active participants in adopting a right way (empowered) of thinking.

My success formula I.T.A.R. is rooted in the physical laws of the universe, and it works synergistically with the Holy Spirit. Our disciplines help place us in a position for the transforming work of Holy Spirit. While Dr. Dweck (and many other scientists) have offered us practical insight into observable patterns of thinking and behavior, we need to always refer back to the ultimate source of insight . . . the Bible.

News flash . . . you don't have to be a Christian to discover the workings (patterns) of the universe. The difference is the nonbeliever observes the same order and design of creation but does not attribute it to the Creator.

The three "Wisdom Books," Proverbs, Ecclesiastes, and Job, all reveal the meaning of life. Proverbs was largely composed by King Solomon (29 of 31 chapters). In 1 Kings 4:32, he is reported to have spoken 3,000 proverbs and written 1,005 songs. Wisdom is a key player in Proverbs.

Since other cultures had recorded Wisdom literature, it's not sure how much Hebrew Wisdom writings were influenced by others. The good news is that it doesn't matter. Observing, recording, and teaching "Wisdom" is owned by no one. God builds it into the fabric of the universe. The huge differentiator is the fact that the Hebrews attributed God as the source.

Proverbs points to *"The fear of the Lord as the beginning of knowledge"* (Proverbs 1:7) and directs us to view all wisdom through the lens of the God who made us.

Note: It is common to hear people today refer to the "universe" as if it were synonymous with God. I take every opportunity (in Love) to carefully point out the fallacy in the thinking, whenever it pops up.

The universe was created by God and is not God!

We discover truths about the physical world we live in (a.k.a., the universe) by the tools God gives us. Check out *Stealing from God: Why Atheists Need God to Make Their Case* by Dr. Frank Turek.

This deception is from the enemy. It's simply a form of *IDOLATRY* and has been with us since the fall of Adam and Eve.

In Ephesians 6:17, Paul tells us to take up the helmet of salvation and sword of the Spirit—which is the word of God. These two pieces of the "Armor of God" instruct us to guard our minds from wrong thinking (helmet) and use God's Word (the Bible) to fight the forces waging war against us (sword).

I want to share with you some practical steps you can use to build up your mind to be more growth-oriented. It's critical to remember to start practicing small, more powerful habits. With greater frequency of use, the habits you practice will become easier and allow you to add bigger empowering habits.

The same is true for eliminating bad habits. Start small, build your muscles (small successes), and go bigger as you gain momentum.

Two Key Ideas:

1. Frequency, not time, is the game changer. Here is a simple example: Which would produce greater results for you, exercising once every 23 days (frequency) for 10 years (time), or exercising 3 X per week (frequency) for 1 year (time)? Both equal about 156 workouts, but only one will achieve the results you're after.

2. Establishing small habits is the best way to start. It should be something that is *easy* for you to do and you are *willing* to do repeatedly. Small successes create a positive feedback loop and help develop momentum in building or breaking habits.

Nine Rules for Shifting to a Growth Mindset

1. Get clear about the areas in which you exhibit a "fixed mindset." You might want to survey a few close friends who will be completely honest with you about what they observe in you.

2. Make a list of your fixed-mindset habits.

3. List a "growth-mindset" habit you want to move to, from each fixed-mindset habit you identified (FM - GM).

4. Make a list of your *I am* statements to support your new habits. Example: If your fixed-mindset habit was to say, "I'm terrible at remembering people's names," you would now make a habit of saying, "I'm getting better at remembering people's names."

5. Post your list in a few places and review them several times a day out loud. This practice is substantially enhanced by visualizing yourself as the new empowered version.

6. Every time you practice the new habit successfully, add a physical expression (clap, shout YES, high-five yourself) to reinforce your behavior. This tiny act of "celebrating the win" releases dopamine in your brain, which makes you feel good and facilitates your desire to repeat.

7. Teach others about FM and GM behaviors. By teaching, your awareness grows and your brain begins to rewire itself.

You will find your self-image improves and your behaviors will reflect this shift.

8. Influences: Surround yourself with better influences: people, books, videos, courses, and mentors/coaches. By increasing the *frequency* and *intensity* of exposure to these positive influences, the faster your mindset changes.

9. Have accountability partners during your journey to keep you on track. If you're married or have a roommate that's willing to help you, make sure you set the ground rules of how you want them to communicate with you.

3. TIME PRIORITY DISCIPLINE

When I first launched my business coaching and consulting, at the beginning of every one-on-one call, I would ask, "What is the biggest challenge you're experiencing that we need to solve?"

The answer nine out of ten times was TIME. "I don't have enough time to get everything done that needs to be done."

I would ask them if people like Oprah, Bill Gates, Jeff Bezos, etc., have more on their plates to do each day than you or I? The answer was always YES.

My next question was this: "How many hours do you have in a day?"

You guessed it, they started to see my point that we all have 24 hours in a day.

The big difference was how they prioritized their time.

Chances are you don't need time management training as much as *you need priority training.*

The main reason some people (Oprah, Gates, Bezos, to name a few) get more done each day than you or me is that they are more focused on their highest-priority activities and less distracted than we are.

Distraction is a main enemy to productivity.

Consider Jeff Bezos. His net worth in 2020 was estimated at $165 billion! He is the founder and CEO of Amazon (just in case you've been living in a cave until now).

Think about his level of productivity on an average day compared to you. How do you think he's able to get so much more done?

I'm sure he doesn't touch his iPhone 2,617 times a day, browse his social media channels to see what interesting things people are posting, binge on the Netflix Original series *Longmire* (OK, I confess, that was me), or check his email 15 times a day. Bezos, like many other highly productive professionals, learned to manage his priorities.

With your permission, I want to take a moment to be your coach (an honor I cherish). Before you start your day, write down the answer to the following question on a piece of paper and review it throughout the day:

What is the Highest and Best Use of my TIME, TALENT, ENERGY, and RESOURCES today?

Highest- and Best-Use Principle

What are you worth per hour? Here's how to figure it out: Divide how much you made last year (net) by the number of hours you worked.

Once you know that hourly figure, prioritize your work so that you only do things that are equivalent to that amount. If your time is worth $100/hour, don't do $20/hour tasks. (Don't get stuck on the dollars per hour; understand the principle.)

I realize that early on in your business, you need to do many things that are below your pay scale because you don't have the finances to pay someone else to do them.

PAY CAREFUL ATTENTION: Too many of you have failed to delegate and elevate at those times *when the resources were available.* This is one of the reasons business growth stalls. This is a *key leverage point.*

Prioritize your time to do those tasks that are the *Highest and Best Use* for you. Delegate everything else to another person or team.

Brian Tracy was one of my business mentors for close to three decades. He has authored dozens of book and training programs in the personal and business development genre. I have read many of his books, listened to his CDs, watched his DVDs, and listened to him live. I love his practical approach to business success. One of his famous statements is "unsuccessful people watch the clock while successful people race the clock." I love this because it describes the mindset of achievement.

As a professional speaker, I had the honor and privilege of sharing the stage with Mr. Tracy (I feel awkward calling him Brian) in 2018. The night before, I sat next to him at dinner and gleaned from his wisdom firsthand. It was a dream come true.

I remember him repeating many of the same lessons he's been teaching for over three decades on successful patterns of time usage. He identified clear differences between how differently time is spent by the more successful people in business.

Here are some of my practices influenced by Brian Tracy's teaching. Remember that tiny habits implemented will compound into consistent powerful behaviors over time.

- I focus on being *Productive* not *Busy*.

- I possess the capacity to improve my time-usage skills.

- My priorities dictate my time and schedule.

- I regularly apply the 80/20 Principle (Pareto). I do my best to focus on the 20 percent of tasks that produce 80 percent of my results.

- I tackle the most difficult task first thing each day.

- I eliminate multitasking and distractions (emails, text messages, social media, unimportant phone calls, etc.).

- I stick to my mantra: "The highest and best use of my time, talent, energy, and resources."

- I leverage my time by delegating to others things not worthy of my time or that I am poorly equipped to do.

- I chunk tasks down into smaller parts and work on them consistently until they're achieved.

- I Say NO to the good in order to achieve the Great!

- I learn fastest by listening to audio teaching. I typically listen at 1.75X speed.

- I Avoid unproductive or low-productive meetings.

- I Respect and control my time, but stay sensitive to being available to the Holy Spirit's direction.

- I Keep an uncluttered workspace.

- I Avoid wasting others' time.

- I convert low-productive time into higher-productive usage—I listen to audiobooks, podcasts, sermons, and other educational materials when I'm working out, driving alone in the car, shopping by myself, in the airport, or on a plane, etc.

Slow Down to Speed Up—God Has a Better Way!

2020 was the year that COVID-19 disrupted everything!

People got ill, some became disabled, and others died as a direct result of this virus. Many believe that the secondary effects of the pandemic were worse.

The global economy was substantially disrupted in a negative way. Some sectors of business were boosted while others seriously suffered.

Fear and anxiety multiplied, exponentially exacerbated by the media and internet.

I saw a different side. Adhering to the general principle that there's "purpose in pain," I asked myself what good could come from this?

Not all who believe in Christ agree with my position that since we believe God is in control, then it stands to reason that He has allowed for this to happen. Maybe He wants to do something great.

Johanna (my wife) and I regularly prayed for all who were walking through trials during this time. Our goal was to focus on the positives. I want to be sensitive to those who were burdened and suffered much pain during this time; I also want to list a few positives I observed:

- More opportunities to share the Gospel with people who were awakened to the brevity of life and the Hope Jesus offers

- A greater appreciation for the things many (including me) took for granted

- More family time

- More people got to know their neighbors better

- More opportunities to relax, pray, and spend time with God

- New ways of doing business (innovation dramatically increased)

- The explosion of online platforms that allow for face-to-face connections and help bridge the "in-person" communication gap

Our decision to look for the opportunities during this time led us to some valuable new lessons and habits. Johanna is heavily involved with our church and serves as part of the leadership team for "small groups" under Julia Mateer. Pastors Julia and Mark Mateer led a six-week leadership training through a book they believed would bless us (I say *us* because spouses of the leadership were included). The book was *The Ruthless Elimination of Hurry* written by Pastor John Mark Comer of Bridgetown Church in Portland, Oregon.

Here are some of my key takeaways:

- In creation, God set a natural biorhythm for us to function by. In Genesis 1:14–18, God gives light to rule the day (the sun) and light to rule the night (the moon). Our natural sleep cycles were designed to follow sunup and sundown.

- The oldest sundial was discovered in Egypt and was believed to have been created around 1500 BC.

- In the sixth century, Saint Benedict organized the monastery around seven times of prayer each day, a superlative idea. By the twelfth century, the monks had invented the mechanical clock to rally the monastery to prayer.

- In 1370, the first public clock tower was erected in Cologne, Germany. Up until then, our rhythms were linked to the rotation of the Earth on its axis and the four seasons. You went to bed with the moon and got up with the sun. Days were long and busy in summer, short and slow in winter. There was a rhythm to the day and even the year. Life was dominated by agrarian rhythms.

- In 1879, Thomas Edison invented the light bulb, which made it possible to stay up past sunset.

- Before Edison's light bulb, the average person slept 11 hours per night. The median number of hours of sleep per night for Americans is down to about seven.

- 2007 was a historic year that massively shifted our time challenges:

  - Steve Jobs (Apple) releases the iPhone

  - Facebook opens to anyone with an email address

  - Twitter becomes its own platform

  - Year one of the "Cloud"

  - The App store is established

  - Intel switches from silicon chips to metal

  - 2007 is the official start of the Digital Age

- The internet and Wi-Fi have become woven into the fabric of most societies

- The smartphone has placed the internet into our pockets

Pastor Comer makes a convincing case, throughout his book, on modeling the "Way" of Jesus by operating our lives with the same habits/disciplines of Jesus. Jesus created margin (fancy lingo for time to be refreshed and reconnect with the Father) in his schedule.

Jesus built "margin" into his schedule.

> *Margin is the space between our load and our limits.*
> *John Mark Comer*

How much margin do you have?

Here's a better way of asking that question. How much downtime are you taking to rest, worship, and reconnect with God?

Jesus often retreated to a place of solitude (Greek: *eremos*) to recharge and reconnect with the Father. This model is seen throughout His ministry and is consistent with the pattern He created in the universe.

You can't pour from an empty cup! Our lives are lived at a pace never before experienced in history. Our margins are eroded if not exhausted.

Consider the Sabbath. Christians have differing opinions on how to keep the Sabbath or whether they should keep it at all.

Consider Genesis 2:1–3, "So the heavens and the earth and everything in them were completed. On the seventh day God had completed his work that he had done, and he rested on the seventh day from all his work that he had done. God blessed the seventh day and declared it holy, for on it he rested from all his work of creation."

Did you ever stop to ask why God rested on the seventh day and blessed it?

Was God tired? I think not. God took time to enjoy all He had made.

Perhaps God was establishing a pattern woven into the fabric of the universe of taking time (one day per week) to stop, rest, worship, fellowship, and devout ourselves to being with our Heavenly Father.

A quote by H. H. Farmer: "If you go against the grain of the universe, you will get splinters."

Could it be that this Sabbath principle benefits us and could actually make us more productive?

When Moses delivered the Ten Commandments to the children of Israel, God was establishing the framework for His people to live by. After all, they had only known the way of Egyptian slavery and all the idolatry from that culture.

In Exodus 20: 8–11, God says:

"Remember the Sabbath day by keeping it holy. Six days you shall labor and do all your work, but the seventh day is a sabbath to the

Lord your God. On it you shall not do any work, neither you, nor your son or daughter, nor your male or female servant, nor your animals, nor any foreigner residing in your towns. For in six days the Lord made the heavens and the earth, the sea, and all that is in them, but he rested on the seventh day. Therefore the Lord blessed the Sabbath day and made it holy."

In Mark 2:27, Jesus tells the Pharisees: *"The Sabbath was made for man and not man for the Sabbath."*

So here is something for us to think about:

- God takes time to enjoy His creation (the Sabbath).

- God reinforces this principle to the Israelites in the Ten Commandments.

- Jesus observes the Sabbath and builds time into His schedule for rest, prayer, and worship.

- Jesus teaches that the Sabbath is for our benefit.

Interestingly, studies have linked productivity declines, increased mistakes and accidents, along with increased work-related injuries from work hours above 50–55 hours per week. (The negative effect of working too many hours varied based on industry.) Check out the 2014 paper by John Pencavel, Professor in the Department of Economics at Stanford University, to see the results supporting these observations on the inverse relationship between work hours and productivity.[1]

The typical work week of 50 hours equates to about six days per week with one day off. Sound familiar?

From the United States Department of Labor:

Long work hours may increase the risk of injuries and accidents and can contribute to poor health and worker fatigue. Studies show

---

1. Pencavel, John *The Economic Journal.* June 2014.

that long work hours can result in increased levels of stress, poor eating habits, lack of physical activity and illness. It is important to recognize the symptoms of worker fatigue and its potential impact on each worker's safety and health and on the safety of co-workers. (*www.osha.gov/SLTC/workerfatigue/hazards.html*)

UNSTOPPABLE TIME SUMMARY

- Focus on being *Productive* not *Busy*.

- Priority management of time usage results in greater productivity in less time.

- Becoming more productive is a skill set that can (and needs) be developed.

- Focus each day on the principle of "*Highest and Best Use.*"

- Build "margin" into your daily life (the space between your load and limits).

- There is Biblical precedent for intervals of work versus rest (six-day work week, one day of rest).

- Science continues to support the relationship of the length of work hours per week (adjusted for industry) and the level of productivity, health, and safety of workers.

- Intentional practice of Sabbath principles is good for our overall well-being and blesses our team members and business profitability.

4. HEALTH AND FITNESS DISCIPLINE

A large popcorn (extra salt please), check; a pint of Starbucks Java Chip ice cream (made by angels), check; frozen Reese's Cups, check; and a large Diet Coke, check. Now I was ready to watch the movie.

From 2005–2009, after selling our restaurants, Johanna and I would go to the movies two to three times per week. I have always been a movie (at the theater) buff as far back as I can remember. I now know that my lifetime addiction to the movies was directly connected to my sugar addiction. Like Pavlov's dogs, the thought of going to the theater, watching the newest releases, and consuming large amounts of empty calories from sugar, salt, and fat caused me to crave the dopamine hit my brain would experience.

Let me paint a clearer picture, I was, up until age 52, a junk food addict. Others had alcohol, drugs, gambling, or cigarettes for their addictions . . . mine was sweets, salt, and fat! I look back at pictures of myself at 52 before my big change, and I see a man on a direct collision course with early heart disease, diabetes, and dementia.

The Bliss Point

Howard Moskowitz graduated from Harvard University in 1969 with a PhD in experimental psychology and was a successful marketing consultant to the food industry. It was Moskowitz that coined the expression *"bliss point"* to capture that perfect amount of sugar, salt, and fat that would send us over the moon with a nice hit of dopamine.

Let's face it, Americans have become the nation of obesity. A 2014 article posted in *U.S. News*, titled "America Tops List of 10 Most Obese Countries," listed the United States as leading the "obesity epidemic." The CDC reports that obesity in America exceeds 42 percent (2017–2018), with 9.2 percent being severely obese. The rates of obesity vary based on age, ethnicity, gender, and socioeconomic status. In 2009, an article was published by Xavier Pi-Sunyer, MD, in the *National Library of Medicine* titled "The Medical Risks of Obesity."

Obesity is a significant risk factor for and contributor to increased morbidity and mortality from:

- cardiovascular disease (CVD)

- diabetes

- cancer

- chronic diseases, including osteoarthritis, liver and kidney disease, sleep apnea, and depression

The American Cancer Society reports that half of all men will develop cancer in their lifetime and one in five will die as a result. Women are less likely to develop cancer (one in three), but one in five will lose their life to this horrible disease.

When it comes to diabetes, the United States also leads the way with about 10 percent of its population between the ages of 20–79 having this dreaded disease. *Note*: Type 2 diabetes (adult onset) is largely preventable.

OK, enough with all these depressing FACTS. What's the point? Now that you asked, let's talk about you! Where would you place yourself on the health spectrum below?

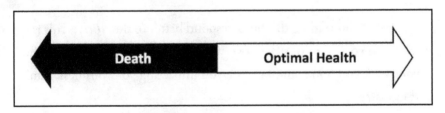

Let me help eliminate the confusion you might be experiencing right now.

We are all going to die some day; however, the bigger question is, what quality of life will we have on our journey?

In the above graphic, I want you to get a grip on your current state and quality of health and which direction you're driving it. The more vibrant your health, the more you stack the deck in your favor in just about everything.

Note: It is challenging to quote scripture that directly addresses our responsibility to steward our health. The good news is, using wise examination of God's Word, we can draw clear direction to the importance of maintaining our health. Consider the following:

Corinthians 6:19–20, "Don't you know that your body is a temple of the Holy Spirit who is in you, whom you have from God? You are not your own, for you were bought at a price. So glorify God with your body."

1 Timothy 4:8, "For bodily exercise is profitable for a little; but godliness is profitable for all things, having promise of the life which now is, and of that which is to come."

Carrot or Stick?

Imagine showing up to your life, walking with God, marriage, family, work, your small group, the gym, etc., every day filled with energy, excitement, and purpose because you're feeling strong and healthy. (That's the *"carrot."*)

Some of you reading this book respond better to the *"stick."* This is for you. When you're out of shape, overweight, fatigued, and depressed, how is your walk with God, and how are you impacting your business, family, and ministry?

Prioritize Your Health

In the Time Discipline section above, I discussed arranging your schedule based on priorities. Your health should be one of those higher priorities.

Look . . . you and I cannot choose our DNA. At conception, our complete set of genes was established. What we can control is our lifestyle.

Epigenetics is the science of how biological mechanisms impact the expression or suppression of genes (how genes are turned on or off, not altered).

Let me give you the "easy to understand" version.

There are things we control and things we don't control that influence how genes are switched on or off. We would all love to control the genes that suppress cancer, heart disease, dementia, diabetes, etc., and turn on the genes that make us thin, strong, mentally sharp, and full of energy. While there is no perfect formula, there are things that can drive the momentum in the direction you desire.

Here are things to consider if you want to know how to stack the deck in your favor:

(*Note*: You should consult your healthcare team for specific advice based on your individual needs. The below items are for educational purposes only.)

- Focus only on the things we can control.

- Keep a positive mindset (growth) (Philippians 4:8).

- Eat healthier

  - Eat locally grown, organic foods as much as possible.

  - Eat a diet with high fiber, quality protein, structured carbs (veggies and fruits), and healthy fats.

- Exercise regularly

  - cardio

  - strength

- balance
- flexibility

- Eliminate or reduce toxic or harmful behaviors
  - smoking
  - alcohol
  - illegal drugs
  - abuse of prescribed medicines

- Daily spiritual practices
  - prayer
  - scripture reading/study
  - meditation
  - worship
  - fellowship
  - service to others

- Commit to learning
  - reading
  - audio
  - video
  - teaching
  - live events

- Be proactive with your health

- Establish your healthcare team (They should be preventative-minded)

  - medical

  - gynecologist (women)

  - urologists (men)

  - dental

  - chiropractic

  - physical therapist

  - massage therapist

  - diet coach

  - trainer

  - acupuncturist

  - natural healing practitioners

- Develop strong social connections (community is key).

- Gut health plays a key role in mental health, immunity, and energy. The gut has been referred to as the *second brain* and is surrounded by a large lymphatic system (think protection against unhealthy microorganisms).

I would heartily recommend for you to take a deep dive into Proverbs. These 31 chapters contain practical (wise) advice on dos and don'ts for greater health, wealth, and happiness (through righteous living). Please remember that, for the most part, Proverbs doesn't point to promises but shows probabilities.

Age 61

OK . . . I picked the wrong parents (one of my standard jokes when speaking on stage).

My dad died in 2018 (he was 85) from what I'll call the "trifecta" . . . heart, kidney, and liver failure. He had two open heart surgeries in his life, and, for most of his adult life, took lots of medicine to regulate problems that could have been helped with diet and exercise (definitely not my dad). Mom is still with us but has had one open heart surgery and one-third of her left lung removed from cancer (many years ago), has atrial fibrillation, and takes a host of medicines.

At 52, I was overweight, and for the most part, not in prime shape. My cholesterol and triglycerides were off the chart (a positive indicator of imminent heart disease) and my health was moving in the wrong direction. When my family doctor recommended I go on a cholesterol-lowering medication, I knew I needed a serious lifestyle change.

I decided to eradicate junk food from my diet and increase my exercise regime. Within a year, I went from 205 pounds to 170, and my cardiac risk profile started reversing. In the past year, I shifted to a more plant-based diet (for greater heart health) and focused on a better combination of cardio, strength training, flexibility, and balance. Unlike my parents, I eat healthy, exercise daily (seven to ten hours per week), and take vitamins and supplements (no meds).

My goal is to live until 105; however, I do have an escape clause built in. On my 104th birthday, I maintain the right to amend my goal!

Eating a healthier diet and daily exercise have substantially boosted my energy, self-image, and my overall sense of well-being. All of this has translated into a better me. The results flow into my spiritual walk, relationships, health, and business.

With great confidence, I can say that "A Better Me (by God's Grace) Has Built a Better Business"!

UNSTOPPABLE HEALTH AND FITNESS SUMMARY

- Focus only the things you can control.
- Your body is a gift from God. Take full responsibility for your health and steward it well.
- You had no choice over your DNA, but you do have choice on how to better influence a healthier expression of it by your lifestyle (diet, exercise, safe and wise behavior).
- Your body weight is a result mostly from your diet. Your fitness level is from a combination of exercise and diet.
- Prioritize your health into your schedule.
- Build a robust healthcare team.
- Develop strong social connections (community is key).
- Start where you're at, do what you can, and live by faith. God Loves You.

5. GENEROSITY DISCIPLINE

I graduated chiropractic college in April 1983. I moved to Sarasota, Florida, found a location to launch my practice, obtained a loan (cosigned by my dad) from a local bank, and opened my doors to the public sometime in the fall.

When I filed my taxes for 1983, I had made . . . drum roll, please . . . a whopping $17,000 (I'm relying on my memory so cut me some slack). It may not sound like much; however, it was the most I had ever made up till then. As my income grew, so did my lifestyle: bigger homes, nicer cars, the newest electronic gadgets, more expensive clothes, etc.

I attended church regularly and tithed. There were two major problems!

First, I did not faithfully tithe nor was I giving much over and above the minimum when I did. Second, and most important, my heart was totally WRONG. I had it completely backwards.

I was building MY EMPIRE and gave God the scraps from MY money that I earned from MY BUSINESS when I felt like it.

WOW, I think back and I'm humbled at my foolish thinking and POOR stewardship.

The Bible is filled, from cover to cover, with God's EXTREME generosity toward us (Romans 5:8) and the command for us to be generous with each other.

Generosity has many facets:

- Financial (money, food, clothing, shelter)

- Physical (service/helping)

- Emotional (listening/understanding)

- Teaching (spreading the Good News of Jesus)

- LOVE and FORGIVENESS

- Patience and tolerance

Here are just a few scriptures to look at:

Acts 20:35, "In all things I have shown you that by working hard in this way we must help the weak and remember the words of the Lord Jesus, how he himself said, 'It is more blessed to give than to receive'" (ESV).

Proverbs 11:24–25, "One gives freely, yet grows all the richer; another withholds what he should give, and only suffers want.

Whoever brings blessing will be enriched, and one who waters will himself be watered" (ESV).

Matthew 6:21, "For where your treasure is, there your heart will be also" (ESV).

1 John 3:17, "But if anyone has the world's goods and sees his brother in need, yet closes his heart against him, how does God's love abide in him?" (ESV).

John 3:16, "For God so loved the world, that he gave his only Son, that whoever believes in him should not perish but have eternal life" (ESV).

Scientific studies continue to support that God "hardwired" us to benefit (be blessed) through the act of giving (generosity).

- Live Longer—Older adult volunteers had a lower risk of dying in a four-year period than non-volunteers (as long as they volunteered for altruistic versus self-oriented reasons), according to a 2012 study in the journal, *Health Psychology*, by Sara Konrath and a team at the University of Michigan.

- Lower Blood Pressure—In a June 2013 study from Carnegie Mellon University, adults over 50 who volunteered at least 200 hours in the past year (four hours per week) were 40 percent less likely to develop high blood pressure than non-volunteers.

- Lower Depression Rates—Americans who donate more than 10 percent of their incomes are less likely to suffer from depression (Generosity Initiative at Notre Dame).

- Excellent Health—Americans who are very giving in relationships are much more likely to be in excellent health (48 percent) than those who are not (31 percent) (Generosity Initiative at Notre Dame).

- Lower Risk of Early Death—Michael J. Poulin, PhD, from the University of Buffalo, found a link between giving and unselfishness and having a lower risk of early death.

Today, I am driven by God's Purpose for my life. I pray daily for His Holy Spirit to keep my heart pure before Him. I am often reminded of the parable of the talents in Matthew 25:14–30. I desire to be faithful with all He has given me (by the way, my wife got this long before I ever did). I am driven to use my time, talents, energies, and resources (loaned to me) to serve Kingdom purposes here on Earth. I'm sending the REAL TREASURE ahead (Matthew 6:19–20).

I want to save you years (perhaps decades) of unwise thinking, wrong motives, and poor stewarding of the resources God has loaned you.

Everything is His!

- Our eternal lives (redeemed by the Lamb)

- Our physical bodies

- Our marriages

- Our children

- Our business

- Our money

- Our time

- Our talents

- Our skill sets

- Our minds

- Our energy

Join me in serving God's purpose. Make the decision that nothing is yours and you are like the servant in Matthew 25. When we stand before the Throne of Grace, God will hold us responsible for what we did with what He gave us.

Make Millions, Steward Wisely, Repeat

In 2019, I attended the National Christian Foundation Annual Conference in Orlando, Florida. Michael Ramsden, President of RZIM (Ravi Zacharias International Ministries), was one of the many amazing speakers. He said something that profoundly impacted my perspective on giving.

Ramsden said, "There are two types of givers: The first gives because there is a need inside them that is filled, while the second type is the person who sees the need someone else has and is compelled to fill it."

This profoundly challenged me. I realized that God has hardwired us to derive benefit from giving, but I want to have a heart that is driven by compassion and love to meet the need others have. I want to give like Jesus gave.

The needs are many! Your tithe (10 percent) belongs to your local church. Giving above your tithe should be led by the Holy Spirit.

In 2 Corinthians 9:6–8, the Apostle Paul tells us to give generously and do it with a cheerful heart.

UNSTOPPABLE GENEROSITY DISCIPLINE SUMMARY

- It's not yours. God owns it all.

- Steward what you've been given so God gets the greatest ROI (return on investment).

- Seek to have a heart like Jesus, so when you give, your primary motivation is filling others' needs.

- Send your treasure ahead. Eternity is a lot longer than life.

- Pray for the Holy Spirit to direct your giving.

- Give generously and with a cheerful heart.

---

6. MASTERY DISCIPLINE

He was reluctant to talk about his professional career playing hockey. He was not terribly proud of the role he played. At 6 ft. 4 in., 225 lb. and a low body fat, Jake was the "enforcer" on his team. When someone on the other team needed to be punished, Jake was put in to accomplish the job.

Jake Taylor was referred to me by a great friend and a former client, Mike Bowen. Mike met Jake through church and was helping him grow in his walk with Jesus.

After leaving hockey, Jake eventually landed in the world of life insurance. He sold specialized life insurance to high net worth individuals to protect their loved ones financially in the unfortunate event of premature death, and at the same time, help them build future wealth when their earning potential was lower.

Like many of my clients, we started working on helping him through my Seven-Step System (modified based on his need) and discovered a much deeper need. Jake was being called to something bigger. While he couldn't quite pinpoint what he wanted, he knew that he was not in love with selling insurance. Something was missing.

If you've ever seen the movie, *The Blind Side,* starring Sandra Bullock, Tim McGraw, and Quinton Aaron as Michael Oher, you'll know the story is about Oher rising from a disadvantaged childhood to the NFL. Like Oher, Jake is hardwired to be a "protector." From protecting his team-mates on the ice, he transitioned into protecting his clients' wealth.

I helped Jake get clear about his past, present, and potential future.

Jake's past as a pro hockey player had prepared him for his current career in life insurance. The problem was his *perspective.* Jake wasn't seeing the tremendous value he was contributing to his current and potential clients. When Jake's father-in-law passed away, his mother-in-law was well cared for because of the wise financial protections put in place. I helped Jake understand that his expertise was helping his clients do the same for their families.

This new view of his role made Jake feel more excited about his current career.

But wait . . . there's more!

This career was preparing Jake for what's next. Maybe you feel there's more for you as well. Track carefully with me because this could be the spark that sets you ablaze.

By asking the right questions and really listening to his heart, taking a deep interest in him as more than a client, I was able to uncover the next part of his journey.

Jake walked through the pain of having to leave professional sports and find meaning and purpose. He described the high of being in the limelight and the status that it came with. He would leave the locker room all showered and dressed after a game only to be inundated by adoring fans. Imagine all the years of climbing the ladder of success in a given area, and with no preparation, it all ends!

Many men and women are forced (voluntarily or involuntarily) from a profession (sports, healthcare, corporate jobs, etc.) into retirement or another role (perceived as lesser status). Adjusting to a life outside of professional sports was very difficult for Jake. His journey has developed a deep understanding for others who have, will, or are currently facing a similar journey.

Jake's previous role as an "enforcer" has emerged as a gift as a "protector." This gift has to be honed into a skill set that allows Jake to serve others in whatever role he's in. This is where mastery comes in.

No success is produced overnight.

It takes years and thousands of hours to develop. The journey is often filled with pain, difficulties, and setbacks. Those who succeed are the ones that persist and push through.

Jake has found two deep needs as a result of his journey:

1. To help other pro athletes move from *pro* to *purpose*.

2. To mentor young athletes (hockey) to develop into who God made them to be—more than an "athlete."

Like Jake, I know the pain of abruptly transitioning at the top of my professional career as a doctor into retirement due to a wrist injury. The adjustment was tough, and it was difficult to see the upside. Jake and I are still in touch, and I hope to play a greater role in helping pros move into their purpose (to be continued . . .).

The discipline of *mastery* takes time, energy, and resources. The results you'll experience will make every challenge you faced along the way worth it!

UNSTOPPABLE MASTERY
SUMMARY

- Mastery is necessary; it separates us from the average.

- The journey to mastery is filled with pain, challenges, and setbacks. These are all needed to develop us into what we need to become.

- Mastery doesn't happen overnight; it takes time, dedication, and lots of work.

- The reward makes it all worthwhile.

- There is purpose in the pain if you look for it.

- God often refines us in the hottest fire, so the impurities can be separated from the character He's developing in us for the purpose He's designed us for.

7. MENTORSHIP DISCIPLINE

One of the greatest values of mentors is the ability to see ahead what others cannot see and to help them navigate a course to their destination.
John C. Maxwell

The location was great, the office was professional looking, the surrounding community was growing, and other practices in the area were doing well, but Bob's wasn't!

Dr. Bob was a nice guy. He was married and had two children. He graduated from the same chiropractic college as I had only several years later. On the outside, it appeared that he had everything he needed to build a thriving practice. So why did he close?

Like so many other business owners, Dr. Bob needed help. He spent years and a small fortune on his education, then even more time and money getting his practice up and running. How could he walk away from all this to take a job in a completely unrelated field to support his family?

Bob was not alone!

Imagine having all the ingredients to make the most magnificent meal but not having the instructions on how to properly create the feast.

Over the past four decades, I have seen far too many good men and women struggle as business owners and

- Fail to make the money they deserve,

- Struggle to make ends meet, and

- Be forced to give up and shut down.

Sometimes it's not their fault. There are extenuating circumstances such as divorce, illness, economic shifts, or legal issues (to name a few) that impact business owners in negative ways. Yet I am deeply saddened by how many businesses could have been saved, and even more prospered, had they only invested in getting the right mentor, coach, or consultant.

The biggest mistake I have seen struggling business owners make is to view business coaching as a cost and not what it really is . . . an investment!

One of my mentors, Armand Morin, is famous for saying, "Success Leaves Traces" (now the title of his book).

Think of what every successful athlete, speaker, actor, singer, musician, pastor, CEO, or business owner has in common—they are the product of what mentors, coaches, teachers, trainers, and consultants have poured into them.

A fool's way is right in his own eyes,
but whoever listens to counsel is wise.
Proverbs 12:15

The difference between success and failure, good or great, average or extraordinary, often depends on one's willingness to invest in continuous personal, professional, and spiritual development.

For business purposes, let's consider the different roles of a coach, mentor, and consultant.

COACH—THE FACILITATOR

- This person helps facilitate the development of personal or professional objectives.

- The coach doesn't provide you with the answers to a challenge or even tell you what to do. Instead, the coach acts as a facilitator to help you ask better questions, and explore your own answers.

- They serve as a guide while you create a plan, define outcomes, and experiment to move your thinking forward. Think "facilitator" and "action-oriented."

MENTOR—THE ADVISOR/TEACHER

- The mentor provides those with less experience advice or assistance in a specific area.

- Mentors may even advise on the skills needed to break through to the next level in a client's career.

- Unlike a coach who helps you discover your own answers, a mentor teaches, sharing their experiences and knowledge on industry-related questions and challenges.

CONSULTANT—PROBLEM SOLVER/IMPLEMENTOR

- The consultant helps answer specific questions or address specific challenges for an organization.

- They provide recommendations based on their own experience, market trends, research, and many other inputs.

- Consultants are often asked to be responsible for implementing those recommendations within the client's organization.

- A key distinction from coaches is that a consultant provides the answer and maybe even becomes responsible for delivering it.

I have been blessed to have built several very successful businesses in different industries over the past four decades.

God deserves the full measure of credit for everything good in my life. He blessed me with great teachers, trainers, coaches, consultants, and mentors.

I have conservatively invested several hundred thousand dollars in growing my personal and business success and the ROI has been exponential.

During the course of writing this book I have invested close to $60,000 in coaching and mentoring. I share this with you, not to impress you but to encourage you because the return on this investment will far exceed the investment.

Let's tackle some *key questions* you might be asking:

Q: Do I need a coach, consultant, or mentor?
A: Chances are, you'll need all three at one time or another. I have found that most of my clients need my help with all three.

Q: When should I hire one?
A: Proactive beats reactive every time! This is one of my core teaching coaching points. Whether you're just starting out, in a building phase, or you've already built a successful business, hiring the right person can help your business grow faster, avoid costly mistakes, negotiate better, build leadership skills, help solve problems, stay on purpose, keep you personally accountable, increase your profitability, and guide you toward financial freedom.

Note: You must be willing to listen, learn, and implement quickly in order to get the most out of your investment. Yes, your mentor/coach/consultant is an investment!

Q: Whom should I hire?
A: You need to know what your greatest needs are first.

- Find someone that shares your core values and vet them to see if they're who they say they are. Puffery is very common.

- Their level of experience is important.

  - Years of experience: Chances are the more years in business, the more experiences they have to draw from.

  - How successful have they been? You wouldn't be wise to hire someone to help you do something they've never done before.

  - What is their personal life like? There are definite red flags you should look out for. For me, I avoid those with personal challenges that could adversely affect their performance (relationship problems, substance abuse, financial issues, integrity challenges).

  - During challenging economic times, it seems like everyone becomes some type of coach, mentor, or consultant.

  - I've seen examples where certain sectors in the economy are moving rapidly upward and many throw their hat into the ring as a self-proclaimed expert. DO YOUR RESEARCH.

- Great mentors are transparent and will let you know if they are the right person for you and vice versa. They will share their success and failures as well.

- Many mentors offer some sort of complimentary exploratory session; however, some charge a fee for their time (chances are they want you to have some skin in the game to see how serious you are).

I have mentors that I've worked with one-on-one, some as part of a group, and others whose programs I've purchased (often more than one), and I have followed their teachings for years. I have living and dead mentors, men and women, older and younger, those who are Christians and some who aren't.

Here is one of the insights I gained while working with them that I find valuable. Once I choose someone to work with, I stick with them, take their advice, and run with it.

Many of you reading this book will want to find someone to help you scale and grow your business faster. I applaud you for the wisdom of investing in both yourself and your business.

Choosing the right person or company to work with you is important. I would encourage you to start by seeking God through the Holy Spirit for direction.

I have designed several special coaching programs for you (the Christian Business Owner) depending on your level of need and the speed of growth you desire.

WANT FASTER RESULTS?

Go to *www.DrRonEccles.com*
to see which coaching program is right for you.

FINAL THOUGHTS

This book is written for Christians who have been called to business ownership. Being an entrepreneur comes with great risks and, if done correctly, great reward.

In the title of this book, you'll notice that *purpose* comes first and *profit* last. This order is intentional.

God gives us life, directs our steps, and allows us to have a business with the potential to generate significant profit. This privilege comes with great responsibility—Godly Stewardship (Matthew 25:14–30).

Our business is a platform to reach people for Christ. In the "Great Commission" (Matthew 28:16–20), we are given our marching orders to make disciples.

Christians who operate their businesses with excellence should expect to receive a healthy ROI. When profits are stewarded properly, wise business owners create a *buffer account* to carry them through leaner times.

The three key ingredients for building a Kingdom-Centered Business are *"The Fuel, The Framework, and The Fire."*

The Fuel describes a life and business primarily focused and dependent on the guidance and power of the Holy Spirit to assist us in following Jesus and glorifying the Father.

The Framework is the "Seven Steps to Building your Seven-Figure Business." This blueprint allows you to establish a *rock-solid foundation* to construct and scale your business to maximum profit with a system that is easy to follow, highly efficient, and mitigates many unnecessary costly mistakes.

The Fire focuses on building a better you. The goal is to develop an "optimized you" that shows up each day in life and business prepared to accomplish the Kingdom assignments you're tasked with.

If you IMPLEMENT everything you learned in this book, I'm confident you'll possess what you need to build the business of your dreams, (whether it's a six- or seven-plus figure).

Let me leave you with seven reminders:

1. Nothing is ours! Our lives and everything we have belong to God.

2. The primary purpose of business ownership is to make disciples.

3. Life is short, eternity is much longer (note my sarcasm). Faithfully steward every gift you've been blessed with (finances, relationships, health, and spiritual).

4. Great businesses are built on purpose. Skills must be intentionally developed and specialized knowledge acquired.

5. Keep perspective. Skillful and diligent work, over time, will typically result in great profit. Use your profit wisely.

6. Great profit without greater purpose is dangerous. Have your accountability team in place in advance.

7. Make investing a way of life. Invest your time, talent, energy, and resources toward building a better business and a better you, and advancing Kingdom work.

WHAT'S NEXT: "THE EIGHTH STEP"

Growing a six- or seven-figure business with purpose, passion, and profit was the goal of this book. I have carefully designed several coaching programs for those wanting faster results.

Once you begin to reap the financial rewards of a successful business you'll need a plan on how to steward the money.

Here are some questions you'll need direction on:

- How much should you give away?

- Where should you give it?

- How should you give it?

- How much should you save?

- How much should you invest?

- What should you invest in?

- What is financial freedom?

- How do you calculate your financial freedom number?

- How do you keep your heart pure from the love of money?

- How to protect your family?

- How do you wisely protect your income from being over taxed?

- How should you plan for retirement?

- How much will you need to live on in your retirement years?

The next book in the Unstoppable Christian Series, *Eighth Step*, will help guide you through these difficult questions. I have leaned on many top experts to help you make more informed decisions. My attempt is to use the Bible as our ultimate source wherever possible.

The goal of this next book is to help you become a better steward and equip you with greater knowledge in order to make you a better steward your finances.

UNSTOPPABLE CHRISTIAN BELIEF STATEMENT

We Believe:

- The Bible is the living Word of God: 2 Timothy 3:16, "All Scripture is breathed out by God and profitable for teaching, for reproof, for correction, and for training in righteousness, that the man of God may be complete, equipped for every good work" (ESV).

- The Apostles' Creed, "I believe in God, the Father Almighty, the Creator of heaven and earth, and in Jesus Christ, his only Son, our Lord; Who was conceived by the Holy Spirit, born of the Virgin Mary, suffered under Pontius Pilate, was crucified, died, and was buried. He descended into the dead. The third day he arose again from the dead. He ascended into heaven and sits at the right hand of God the Father Almighty, whence he shall come to judge the living and the dead. I believe in the Holy Spirit, the holy universal Church, the communion of saints, the forgiveness of sins, the resurrection of the body, and the life everlasting. Amen."

- God will hold us accountable for how we steward what we've been given: Matthew 25:14–30, "For it will be like a man going on a journey, who called his servants and entrusted to them his property. To one he gave five talents, to another two, to another one, to each according to his ability. Then he went away. He who had received the five talents went at once and traded with them, and he made five talents more. So also he who had the two talents made two talents more. But he who had received the one talent went and dug in the ground and hid his master's money. Now after a long time the master of those servants came and settled accounts with them. And he who had received the five talents came forward, bringing five talents more, saying, 'Master, you delivered to me five talents; here, I have made five talents more.' His master said to him, 'Well done, good and faithful servant. You have been faithful over a little; I will set you over much. Enter into the joy of your master.' And he also who had the two talents came forward, saying, 'Master, you delivered to me two talents; here, I have made two talents more.' His master said to him, 'Well done, good and faithful servant. You have been faithful over a little; I will set you over much. Enter into the joy of your master.' He also who had received the one talent came forward, saying, 'Master, I knew you to be a hard man, reaping where you did not sow, and gathering where you scattered no seed, so I was afraid, and I went and hid your talent in the ground. Here, you have what is yours.' But his master answered him, 'You wicked and slothful servant! You knew that I reap where I have not sown and gather where I scattered no seed? Then you ought to have invested my money with the bankers, and at my coming I should have received what was my own with interest. So take the talent from him and give it to him who has the ten talents. For to everyone who has will more be given, and he will have an abundance. But from the one who has not, even what he has will be taken away. And cast the worthless servant into the outer darkness. In that place there will be weeping and gnashing of teeth.'" (ESV).

- The goal of our *stewardship* is to be found faithful: 1 Corinthians 4:2, "Moreover, it is required of stewards that they be found faithful" (ESV).

- The Bible clearly teaches that suffering, trials, difficulties, and death are all part of our journey: James 1:2, "Count it all joy, my brothers, when you meet trials of various kinds" (ESV).

- In the power of the Holy Spirit—It is only through God's Holy Spirit that we have victory over the flesh: Romans 8:1–9, "There is therefore now no condemnation for those who are in Christ Jesus. For the law of the Spirit of life has set you free in Christ Jesus from the law of sin and death. For God has done what the law, weakened by the flesh, could not do. By sending his own Son in the likeness of sinful flesh and for sin, he condemned sin in the flesh, in order that the righteous requirement of the law might be fulfilled in us, who walk not according to the flesh but according to the Spirit. For those who live according to the flesh set their minds on the things of the flesh, but those who live according to the Spirit set their minds on the things of the Spirit. For to set the mind on the flesh is death, but to set the mind on the Spirit is life and peace. For the mind that is set on the flesh is hostile to God, for it does not submit to God's law; indeed, it cannot. Those who are in the flesh cannot please God. You, however, are not in the flesh but in the Spirit, if in fact the Spirit of God dwells in you. Anyone who does not have the Spirit of Christ does not belong to him" (ESV).

- God is still in the miracle working business. God is working in our lives in both supernatural (miracles) and natural ways. *Miracles: The Credibility of New Testament Accounts* by Craig Keener

- Faith is a necessary ingredient to a victorious life: Hebrews 11:6, "And without faith it is impossible to please him, for whoever would draw near to God must believe that he exists and that he rewards those who seek him" (ESV).

- It is "God's Will" that we need to align with and not the other way around: Proverbs 3:5, "Trust in the Lord with all your heart, and do not lean on your own understanding" (ESV).

- God blesses his people with different gifts and abilities to be used for Kingdom purposes: Romans 12:6–8, "Having gifts that differ according to the grace given to us, let us use them: if prophecy, in proportion to our faith; if service, in our serving; the one who teaches, in his teaching; the one who exhorts, in his exhortation; the one who contributes, in generosity; the one who leads, with zeal; the one who does acts of mercy, with cheerfulness" (ESV).

- Grace and Love need to cover our differences, provided we remain within the fundamentals of Christian Doctrine (Apostles' Creed)

- Certain people (not everyone) are called to be business owners (entrepreneurs)

- Being a Christian doesn't guarantee your financial success in business (or life)

- There are people within the church that abuse the Word of God, by twisting it or taking it out of context for financial gain. We must be discerning (distinguish Truth from almost-truth): 1 John 4:1, "Beloved, do not believe every spirit, but test the spirits to see whether they are from God, for many false prophets have gone out into the world" (ESV).

- We are each responsible to study the Word of God and always be prepared to give an answer for what we believe: 1 Peter 3:15, "but in your hearts honor Christ the Lord as holy, always being prepared to make a defense to anyone who asks you for a reason for the hope that is in you; yet do it with gentleness and respect" (ESV).

- God calls all believers to place the higher priority of "storing treasures (wealth) in heaven" over creating worldly wealth: Matthew 6:19, "Do not lay up for yourselves treasures on earth, where moth and rust destroy and where thieves break in and steal" (ESV).

- Business owners are marketplace evangelists. If we excel at what we do, operate our business on solid fundamentals, and steward our profits, we can be very wealthy (no guarantee). We are responsible for all that we receive: Colossians 3:23–24, "Whatever you do, work heartily, as for the Lord and not for men, knowing that from the Lord you will receive the inheritance as your reward. You are serving the Lord Christ" (ESV).

- We should guard our hearts, minds, and lips from criticizing our Christian brothers and sisters who have different views and practices from ours. Let's first put our own hearts in check: Matthew 7:3, "Why do you see the speck that is in your brother's eye, but do not notice the log that is in your own eye?" (ESV).

- False prophets and teachings need to be exposed and warned against: Matthew 7:15, "Beware of false prophets, who come to you in sheep's clothing but inwardly are ravenous wolves" (ESV).

- CAUTION: Beware of being self-righteous. Discern carefully with the guidance of the Holy Spirit and, above all, act with Love and Grace. 1 Corinthians 16:14, "Let all that you do be done in love" (ESV).

ABOUT THE AUTHOR

Dr. Ron Eccles is, first and foremost, a servant of God, a husband, father, grandfather, accomplished speaker, author, and business consultant. Since 1983, he has owned and operated multiple successful businesses.

He grew up in a blue collar family in New Jersey, finishing his undergraduate studies at Trenton State College in 1979. Graduating from Logan College of Chiropractic in Chesterfield, Missouri, in 1983, he established his private practice in Sarasota, Florida. In the following decade, he was board certified in Chiropractic Orthopedics and Neurology.

Retiring from full-time practice in 1993 due to an injury, Dr. Ron began teaching postgraduate courses for several Chiropractic Colleges in the fields of orthopedics, neurology, impairment rating, and whiplash.

In the mid '90s, he became a restaurateur, owning and operating multiple restaurants before turning his expertise to investing in real estate. From the world of real estate investing, his passion for motivational speaking, business coaching, and teaching gradually emerged.

He was labeled "The Success Doctor" because of his commitment to studying successful people, businesses, and principles since 1980.

Dr. Ron has built a strong reputation for his relentless pursuit of excellence, integrity, and teaching since 2008. He has emceed over 50 events, spoken on more than 100 stages, and influenced tens of thousands of entrepreneurs.

Ron and his wife, Johanna, cofounded "Unstoppable Christian Worldwide" and ROAR. These "Businesses as Ministries" are currently serving the Christian body.

Today, Ron has dedicated most of his time to coaching, teaching, and mentoring Christian Business Owners. Johanna and Ron have five children and three grandchildren. They live on the Gulf Coast of Florida and are active members of Bayside Community Church in Bradenton.

Please check out *www.DrRonEccles.com* to discover how to get involved in one of his coaching programs or to hire Dr. Ron to speak.

A free ebook edition is available with the purchase of this book.

To claim your free ebook edition:

1. Visit MorganJamesBOGO.com
2. Sign your name CLEARLY in the space
3. Complete the form and submit a photo of the entire copyright page
4. You or your friend can download the ebook to your preferred device

Morgan James BOGO™

A **FREE** ebook edition is available for you or a friend with the purchase of this print book.

CLEARLY SIGN YOUR NAME ABOVE

Instructions to claim your free ebook edition:
1. Visit MorganJamesBOGO.com
2. Sign your name CLEARLY in the space above
3. Complete the form and submit a photo of this entire page
4. You or your friend can download the ebook to your preferred device

Print & Digital Together Forever.

Snap a photo

Free ebook

Read anywhere

CPSIA information can be obtained
at www.ICGtesting.com
Printed in the USA
JSHW041417180322
24008JS00001B/11